// **MUSCULAR FAITH** //

HOW TO STRENGTHEN
YOUR HEART, SOUL,
AND MIND FOR THE
ONLY CHALLENGE THAT MATTERS

MUSCULAR FAITH

BEN PATTERSON

SALTRIVER®
AN IMPRINT OF TYNDALE HOUSE PUBLISHERS, INC., CAROL STREAM, ILLINOIS

Visit Tyndale online at www.tyndale.com.

TYNDALE is a registered trademark of Tyndale House Publishers, Inc.

SaltRiver and the SaltRiver logo are registered trademarks of Tyndale House Publishers, Inc.

Muscular Faith: How to Strengthen Your Heart, Soul, and Mind for the Only Challenge That Matters

Designed by Erik M. Peterson

Published in association with the literary agency of Credo Communications, LLC, Grand Rapids, MI 49525; www.credocommunications.net.

Library of Congress Cataloging-in-Publication Data

Patterson, Ben, date.
   Muscular faith : how to strengthen your heart, soul, and mind for the only challenge that matters / Ben Patterson.
     p. cm.
   Includes bibliographical references (p.   ).
   ISBN 978-1-4143-1666-6 (sc)
1. Christian life. I. Title.
   BV4501.3.P383 2011
   248.4—dc22
                                                    2011016088

Printed in the United States of America

17   16   15   14   13   12   11
 7   6   5   4   3   2   1

DEDICATED TO THE MEMORY OF
JAMES STEWART EVANS

CONTENTS

PART 4 // THE ESSENTIALS 129
How to Fight the Good Fight

INTRODUCTION

A FAITH WORTH FIGHTING FOR

Christianity, if false, is of no importance, and, if true, is of infinite importance. The one thing it cannot be is moderately important.
C. S. LEWIS, "CHRISTIAN APOLOGETICS"

You take over. I'm about to die, my life an offering on God's altar. This is the only race worth running. I've run hard right to the finish, believed all the way. All that's left now is the shouting—God's applause! Depend on it, he's an honest judge. He'll do right not only by me, but by everyone eager for his coming.
2 TIMOTHY 4:6-8, *THE MESSAGE*

FOR THE PAST fifteen years or so, I've been a campus pastor, so I've watched hundreds of first-year students arrive on campus fresh faced and bright eyed for fall orientation weekend. These young men and women are nervously hopeful; they are eager to grow and make friends, get a college degree, discover a vocation and a calling in life, and maybe even find a spouse. I watch them and pray for them with a fatherly longing in my heart.

As they step out on their own, imperceptible trajectories are being set and adjusted. The differences in direction seem so tiny and insignificant in the moment, but years in the future they will be gigantic, the way a ship leaving San Francisco harbor for Honolulu, slightly off course, may end up in Shanghai instead. But seaports have no eternal consequence; the direction of a life does.

I'm aware, in ways they can't yet be, that some of the decisions these young people are making now will set the course for their lives. That's largely because I'm much closer to the finish line than they are. I feel about my age like Lou Holtz felt when he coached football at the University of Arkansas. He said of that Southern state, "It's not the end of the world, but you can see it from here."

I live with a great deal of curiosity about how I'm going to turn out in the end. It's because of a very unscientific theory I have about old age. I believe that when life has whittled us down, when joints have failed and skin has wrinkled and capillaries have clogged and hardened, what is left of us will be what we were becoming all along, in our essence.

Exhibit A is a distant relative of mine. For the sake of family pride, I'll give him an alias—Ray. All his life he did nothing but find new ways to get rich. A few of his schemes succeeded, and he became a moderately wealthy man. He spent his senescence very comfortably, drooling and babbling constantly about all the money he had made. I remember watching when I was a child and even then being dumb-struck that he had wasted his whole life getting something that was useless to him as he approached eternity. It was worse than useless—it was an impediment. When life whittled him down to his essence, all that was left was raw greed. That was the man Ray had cultivated in a thousand little ways over a lifetime. He was a living illustration of the adage "The reason men and rivers are crooked is that both take the line of least resistance."

Exhibit B is my wife's grandmother. No need to protect family pride with her. Her name was Edna. When she died in her mid-eighties, she had already been senile for several years. What did this lady talk about? The best example I can think of was what happened when we asked her to pray before dinner. She would reach out and hold the hands of those sitting beside her; a broad beatific smile would spread across her face; her dim eyes would fill up with tears as she looked up to heaven; and her chin would quaver as she poured out her love for Jesus. That was Edna in a nutshell. She loved Jesus, and she loved people. She couldn't remember our names, but she couldn't keep her hands from patting us lovingly whenever we got near her. When life whittled her down to her essence, all that was left was love. That was the woman Edna had cultivated over years by thousands of little acts of love. Her life wasn't easy; she had to fight for love and joy amid some great and terrible disappointments. But she fought—and made a strong finish.[1]

THE NOBLE WARRIOR

The apostle Paul also finished well. Near the end of his life he wrote something I dearly want to be able to say at my end. Tradition says he was beheaded in Rome, not long after he wrote these words:

As for me, my life has already been poured out as an offering to God. The time of my death is near. I have

*fought the good fight, I have finished the race, and
I have remained faithful. And now the prize awaits
me—the crown of righteousness, which the Lord, the
righteous Judge, will give me on the day of his return.
And the prize is not just for me but for all who eagerly
look forward to his appearing.* (2 Timothy 4:6-8)

Not that it matters, but I am sure he looked exactly the
way the apocryphal *Acts of Paul* described him about a hundred years after his death:

[He was] a little man with a big, bold head. His
legs were crooked, but his bearing was noble. His
eyebrows grew close together and he had a big nose.
A man who breathed friendliness.[2]

I love this man. I mean, there he was in a Roman prison, ach-
ing and old but still running and fighting. Moses, speaking
of the great mass of humanity, said we "[end] our years with
a groan" (Psalm 90:9). Not Paul, that old warhorse. The man
with the big nose ended his years with a snort and a kick,
breathing friendliness.

Paul's faith vocabulary was robust and energetic.
From the day of his conversion on, he lived in conflict
and struggle. But Paul cheerfully thought of the Christian
life as being "poured out," as fighting a good fight, finishing
a race, and winning a prize—just like his Lord did. He got
his vocabulary from Jesus, who said the same thing, using

the same word for fighting and fight. Jesus declared that one must enter the Kingdom of God the way a wrestler wrestles, a warrior wages war, and a runner runs a race. The Greek word was *agon*, from which we get our English word *agony*.

Paul and Edna had a muscular faith. The arenas they fought in were different, but their faith was the same. Muscular faith is not a specialized kind of faith, suited only to certain personalities and temperaments. Muscular faith is simply biblical faith, which by definition is vigorous and demanding, for it requires that you stake your whole existence on God and trust in him as your only hope. And this is critical: Muscular faith is not what God demands of you in order to be accepted into his Kingdom; it is the kind of life you live in his Kingdom. To shirk a vigorous faith is to refuse the kind of life Christ calls you to and teaches you how to live. Jesus invited the weary and overburdened to come into his fellowship and learn from him. The life he promised he described as a kind of yoke that would fit his followers. He even called it "light." But he never said it would be passive.

> Muscular faith is not what God demands of you in order to be accepted into his Kingdom; it is the kind of life you live in his Kingdom.

WALKING THE RAZOR EDGE

Because I work with college students, I have a foot in two worlds. They are in their teens and twenties, and I am in my sixties. I'm thinking about my ending, while they're trying to figure out their beginning. But the differences are superficial. We both want to commit our lives to something of supreme worth. And we are both very interested in the future—where we are headed, or should be headed, and how we are going to turn out. So much is riding on where we end, on where our life's trajectory takes us! C. S. Lewis lays out the two possible outcomes:

> [For] in some sense, as dark to the intellect as it is unendurable to the feelings, we can be both banished from the presence of Him who is present everywhere and erased from the knowledge of Him who knows all. We can be left utterly and absolutely *outside*—repelled, exiled, estranged, finally and unspeakably ignored. On the other hand, we can be called in, welcomed, received, acknowledged. We walk every day on the razor edge between these two incredible possibilities.[3]

This book is about what it means to live "on the razor edge between these two incredible possibilities." It assumes that our faith is not something to which we casually assent but something for which we must fight. In our relatively peaceful and prosperous part of the globe, the idea of "muscular faith" may sound a bit overblown. But why then did Jesus speak so urgently about finding the narrow path and being willing to lay down our lives? As I've walked my own sixty-odd years of faith, I've learned a bit and thought a lot about the obstacles to faith all of us face and, I'm happy to report, the unseen yet strength-giving essentials God provides to all those who commit to following Jesus.

One of the first men to model strength and protection in that way was my scoutmaster. As I got ready to go to Boy Scout camp for the first time, I was excited to learn there was a pool in the mountains where we would swim every day.

What a welcome change that would be from my experience at the one public pool in my neighborhood in South Central Los Angeles. As I recall, it was called the Compton Municipal Plunge. But one rarely plunged into the Plunge, it was so packed with the bodies of kids.

My buddies and I would practice "swimming" there. Even if we had actually known how to swim, it would not have been possible because the pool was so crowded. But we did our best to imitate what we had seen the real swimmers do, mostly Johnny Weissmuller in Tarzan movies. I would kick and stroke in the three or four feet of space I had, and it kind of felt like I was swimming. Yes, it truly did feel like I must be swimming. My buddies would do the same thing and get the same sensation. After a summer of this, we congratulated ourselves on our skill as swimmers. Deep in our minds we knew we really couldn't swim, but if anyone asked us, we would declare that we could. I remember coming home one day and announcing to my family that I had learned to swim. They were delighted. I must have been ten or eleven years old.

How wonderful it would be to share the pool at camp with just a dozen or so of my fellow Scouts. The first morning of camp, my scoutmaster asked me if I could swim.

"Yes," I lied.

He said, "Good. Then you'll have no problem passing the swim test."

"What swim test?" I asked.

"Just swim the length of the pool—should be easy for a swimmer," he answered.

But I wasn't a swimmer. And now I would be found out as the fraud I knew myself to be, while I drowned in the swim test! I cried as I confessed my lie to my scoutmaster. I cried even more as I contemplated a week at camp watching all the other boys swim while I sat hot and dirty outside the fence around the pool.

My scoutmaster was a good man. He smiled and said, "Why don't you try?"

"But I can't," I sobbed.

"Just try it," he said.

"But I'll sink and drown," I moaned.

"Tell you what I'll do," he said. "I'll make sure you swim in the outside lane, and I'll walk alongside you on the deck. If you start to sink, I'll reach down and pull you out. All you have to do is jump in and try."

I had to think about that. I wasn't sure what would be worse—drowning or being rescued in front of all the other Scouts. But I decided to trust his plan.

Later that afternoon I stood with ten other little boys at

the deep end of the pool. The deep end! We'd have to start there and swim the twenty-five yards to the shallow end. Why couldn't we start in the shallow end? I wore big green boxer-style swim trunks that were a size too large. The bow on the white drawstring protruded over the top of my trunks. I remember shivering in the hot sun and noticing for the first time in my young life that my legs were skinny and exceptionally white—like the drawstring.

My scoutmaster was watching me with a steady gaze and smiling. At the signal, I jumped in and sank to the bottom of the pool. All the way to the bottom. I had no idea that a human being could sink so deep in water. From the shadowy depths, I looked up at the light from the sun shimmering on the pool's surface, way, way up there, and could see the form of my scoutmaster to my right. Slowly, slowly I rose to the surface and gasped for air. With one big gulp of precious oxygen in my lungs, I started thrashing out strokes in the water. I couldn't seem to get my nose far enough out of the water to breathe again, so I held my breath and labored and lunged forward. I looked over at my scoutmaster and saw that he was still there. This was the hardest thing I had ever done. But I was moving forward, and though it seemed to take forever, I finished the test! And there was my scoutmaster at the end, helping me out of the water. Boy Scout campout saved! Little Boy Scout's confidence restored! Good scoutmaster!

Life has gotten so much more complicated and difficult since then. But it has never felt harder than it did that day to that scared little boy. So my world was small, but it was my world and it was all I knew. Even as it seemed to be falling apart and I was sinking, someone came along and called me to do a very hard thing, something that would require all I had. My all would not be enough, but if he went with me, it would. No muscle was needed outside the pool. It took no muscle to jump in. But once the plunge was made, life in the pool would take muscle—muscular faith—trust in the good scoutmaster.

It will be a fight—savage at times—to finish life well; for our enemies are legion and our strength is small. Great courage and determination are required, more than any of us have. But God's grace is abundant—all we will ever need—and the reward far outweighs the cost.

"The command of Jesus is hard, unutterably hard, for those who try to resist it," wrote Dietrich Bonhoeffer. "But for those who willingly submit, the yoke is easy, and the burden is light. . . . Jesus asks nothing of us without giving us the strength to perform it."[4]

PART 1

THE CALL TO A VIGOROUS FAITH

TO FIGHT THE GOOD FIGHT AND FINISH THE RACE

CHAPTER 1

THE CALL

THE GOOD HARD

I have fought the good fight, I have finished the race, and I have
remained faithful.
2 TIMOTHY 4:7

Grace is opposed to merit, but it is not opposed to effort.
BRADLEY NASSIF

THE SEEDS FOR this book were planted when I was five years
old.

There was a bully in my neighborhood, a really big kid,
maybe seven or eight years old, who could ride a two-wheel
bicycle. None of my friends or I could do this, so we held
him in awe, and he knew it. Whenever my buddies and I
would play a game on the sidewalk, he'd get on his two-
wheeler bicycle and ride as fast as he could, right down the
middle of the sidewalk in our direction, screaming for us
to *move!* He was terrifying on that big two-wheeler, and we
scrambled frantically to get out of his way.

But with each humiliation my resentment grew. I didn't
know what the word *injustice* meant, but I was learning what
it felt like. It wasn't right that he had his fun by bullying us.
So one day I decided not to move when he bore down on us

at top speed. I stood up, planted my feet, and faced him, tall and righteous and proud. He ran over me. Two things stand out in my memory of the collision. One was the surprise I felt at how much it hurt to get run over. The other was that he got hurt too, even more than I did. The impact had also sent him crashing to the pavement. I remember lying on the sidewalk, my breath knocked out of me, gasping for air, unable even to cry. That was bad; it was the most pain I had ever experienced in my young life. But I heard him *wailing* in pain and rage! And when I looked, I saw him lying a few feet away, his knees skinned up and his forehead bleeding. That was good! And it got even better when I saw his mother, who had witnessed the whole incident, run over and scold him for what he had done.

LIFE IS TOUGHER IF YOU'RE STUPID

I limped home in triumph, with the germ of an idea in my mind that I've reflected on ever since. What I did was hard to do, so hard that I'd think twice before I did it again. But what I had been suffering at the hands of that little terrorist was hard too, harder actually. The choice had not been whether to do a hard thing, but which hard thing—the good hard or the bad hard. That brings to mind an old World War II movie in which a Marine Corps drill instructor tells a lazy recruit, "Life is tough, son. But it's a lot tougher if you're stupid." Better to sweat and strain in basic training than to end up dead in combat.

Life is hard. The question is not whether it will be hard but in what way. My friend has a poster of Dan Gable—perhaps the greatest Olympic wrestler of all time—in his basement. The poster shows him straining and sweating as he lifts weights. His face is etched with pain; the veins on his neck and arms are bulging. The caption reads, "There are two kinds of pain: the pain of discipline or the pain of regret." There is good hardness and bad hardness, the pain of living wisely and the greater pain of living foolishly. We can choose which one it will be. Good hard is often hard at the beginning but easier in the end. Bad hard usually begins easy but is hard in the end—sometimes hellish, literally hellish.

The question is not whether life will be hard but in what way.

For this reason Jesus urged people to choose good hardness. He was once asked, "Lord, will only a few be saved?" (Luke 13:23).

He answered the question the way he answered most questions—by not answering it. Apparently Jesus didn't think much of the questions people asked. He knew the power of questions to determine answers (like the old comic line, "When are you going to stop beating your wife?"). The question was a bad question because it begged the real question, which was not "How many will be saved?" but rather "How does *anyone* get saved?" It probably also revealed a smug complacency in the person who asked it, an attitude that was really asking, "How many do you think will be with me in heaven?"

AGON

So Jesus redefined the terms of the discussion and answered, "Work hard to enter the narrow door to God's Kingdom, for many will try to enter but will fail" (Luke 13:24).

The Greek verb translated "work hard" is a dynamically forceful and demanding word. Other translations render it "strive" (ESV, NASB) or "make every effort" (NIV). Actually, the root of the verb is a noun, *agon*, which first referred to "a place of assembly" and then morphed into "a place of conflict," as in the stadium where athletic contests took place, especially contact sports like boxing and wrestling.[1] But over time, the place where people went to see the fights, the *agon*, became the name for the fighting that went on there.

Agon is the word for the gritty, sweaty struggle athletes throw themselves into when they square off and fight; it embodies the grunts and fierce earnestness they bring to the boxing ring, the wrestling mat, the football field. *Agon* is a word one can almost hear and smell. It is a word for the good hard, the good fight of combat on the athletic field or battlefield, and it is a metaphor Jesus used to describe what is required for entry into his Kingdom.

Is salvation a free gift, or is it hard work? Sometimes the Bible seems to contradict itself. Depending upon how one thinks about these things, the writers of the Bible—in this case, Paul and Jesus—seem to disagree. How does each answer the critical, all-important question: Is salvation a gift or an achievement, an award for merit or an act of mercy?

Does God give us eternal life because of the good things we have done or in spite of the bad things we have done? Depending on where one reads in the New Testament, it can seem to be either one or the other. For instance, in one place, Paul wrote, "God saved you by his grace when you believed. And you can't take credit for this; it is a gift from God. Salvation is not a reward for the good things we have done, so none of us can boast about it" (Ephesians 2:8-9).

The apostle Paul's answer is easy to like. What's not to like about salvation being a gift? The Lord's answer is something else; it seems to cast the whole question of salvation by grace in grave doubt. How are we to reconcile Paul's assertion that salvation is a gift with Jesus' words? "Work hard to enter the narrow door to God's Kingdom, for many will try to enter but will fail." In another place Jesus said, "You can enter God's Kingdom only through the narrow gate. The highway to hell is broad, and its gate is wide for the many who choose that way. But the gateway to life is very narrow and the road is difficult, and only a few ever find it" (Matthew 7:13-14).

GOD'S GOOD HARD WORK, HARD AT WORK

Who can do this? Who can walk the hard and narrow way and fight the good fight? I can't. I've failed too many times to think I can. Is Paul saying one thing and Jesus another? No, taken together, both are saying the same thing: that we are not saved by *our* hard work, but by *God's* hard work, hard at work within us. For although grace rules out human merit, it stimulates great, even heroic human effort.[2] In fact, Paul himself provides the Bible's most succinct and epigrammatic statement of this principle in his letter to the Philippians, where he tells us to work out what God works into us:

> *Therefore, my dear friends, as you have always obeyed—not only in my presence, but now much more in my absence—continue to work out your salvation with fear and trembling, for it is God who works in you to will and to act in order to fulfill his good purpose.* (Philippians 2:12-13, NIV)

What does God work in us? First he works our salvation: Christ died for our sins. When we were powerless to help ourselves, Christ died for the ungodly, the just for the unjust. God was in Christ reconciling the world to himself, not counting our sins against us (see Romans 5:6-8; 2 Corinthians 5:19). All of this was done entirely on his initiative. But it didn't stop there; he not only worked to save us, he works in us, by his Spirit, to make us want to be saved. That's how bad off we are without his illuminating and enlivening Spirit—we are dead in sins and trespasses. The dead don't know anything because part of what it means to be dead is not to know you are dead! We would not even want him, who is our life, if he didn't stir us in our spiritual graves (see Ephesians 2:1-10).

> Christ not only worked to save us, he works in us, by his Spirit, to make us want to be saved.

8

And as if all that were not enough, he continues to work in us to bring our salvation to completion: "God, who began the good work within you, will continue his work until it is finally finished on the day when Christ Jesus returns" (Philippians 1:6). Our salvation has a past, present, and future, and in every tense it is the gift of the God "who always was, who is, and who is still to come" (Revelation 4:8).

ONLY TWO RELIGIONS

When Dr. Harry Ironside finished preaching the gospel to a university audience in California, he was approached by a student who asked, "Dr. Ironside, there are literally thousands of religions in the world. How can we know which one of these is true?" Ironside replied:

> Well, before we can get into the question of which one is true, we need to clarify something. There are not thousands of religions. There are not even hundreds of religions. There are only two: one which tells you that salvation comes as a reward for what you have done, and one which tells you that salvation comes by what somebody else does for you. That's Christianity. All the rest fit under the other. And if you think you can get your salvation by your own efforts, then Christianity has nothing to say to you. But if you know you need to be saved, then you are a candidate.[3]

There has never been anything *we* can do to be saved, we *can* do to be saved, or we can *do* to be saved. Salvation comes only by God's grace through faith in Christ. Yet the apostle Paul, Mr. Grace himself, says to "work out your salvation with fear and trembling" (NIV). The Greek word for "work out" carries the idea of bringing to completion, or as the New Living Translation renders the meaning of this line, we are to "work hard to show the *results* of [our] salvation, obeying God with deep reverence and fear. For God is working in [us], giving [us] the desire and the power to do what pleases him" (Philippians 2:12-13, italics mine).

Paul says to work hard because God is giving us both the desire to work hard and the power to do so. By implication, not to work hard would be to work against the very grace that saves us. Our salvation is both a gift from God, a completed act—and a process in which we are strenuously involved. Sometimes Paul's strenuous involvement, his *agon*, was so consuming that his words almost trip over each other when he tries to explain it: "But whatever I am now, it is all because God poured out his special favor on me—and not without results. For I have worked harder than any of the other apostles; yet it was not I but God who was working through me by his grace" (1 Corinthians 15:10).

GOD'S MASTERPIECE

Paul worked hard because God had worked hard on him. He didn't obey in order to be saved; he obeyed because he was saved. Obedience is the purpose and the goal of salvation. Or as Paul puts it in his classic text on salvation by grace alone through faith alone, "Salvation is not a reward for the good things we have done, so none of us can boast about it. *For we are God's masterpiece*. He has created us anew in Christ Jesus, so we can do the good things he planned for us long ago" (Ephesians 2:9-10, italics mine).

God has "created us anew"—given us new birth "so we can do the good things he planned for us long ago." Again, we don't do good things in order to be saved; we do good things because we are saved. We are not born again *by* good works; we are born again *for* good works. Paul says the intent of all this grace is to make us "God's masterpiece." Since we are God's masterpiece, we not only should act like a masterpiece, we now *may* act in the power of the God who is making us so.

We are not born again *by* good works; we are born again *for* good works.

The great Renaissance artist Leonardo da Vinci was hard at work on a canvas he had been toiling over for weeks. The painting was nearly finished and looked magnificent. The subject had been carefully chosen, and it had da Vinci's unique perspective and distinctive choice of colors. Suddenly he stopped, called a student over, handed him the paintbrush, and said, "Here, you finish it." The student protested that he was not worthy or able to complete so beautiful a painting.

Said da Vinci, "Will not what I have done inspire you to do your best?"

That is a little bit like the thing God's grace does in us, except God does much more than give us an inspiring model; he gives us his Spirit to live in us, as he promised through the prophet Ezekiel: "And I will give you a new heart, and I will put a new spirit in you. I will take out your stony, stubborn heart and give you a tender, responsive heart. And I will put my Spirit in you so that you will follow my decrees and be careful to obey my regulations" (Ezekiel 36:26-27).

The gospel of God's grace implacably opposes any notion of human merit for salvation, but it embraces and commands vigorous effort, good hard work for the saved. We are to strenuously work out what God has graciously worked in. This is why Christ came. When St. Athanasius wrote, "God became human that humans might become divine," he was echoing the apostle John, who wrote, "Dear friends, we are already God's children, but he has not yet shown us what we will be like when Christ appears. But we do know that we will be like him, for we will see him as he really is" (1 John 3:2). And so St. Augustine prayed, "My God, set me on fire! . . . Give what you command, and then command whatever you will."[4]

SPIRITUAL DNA

I have an athletic fantasy that I occasionally roll over in my mind during football season. In it, I am the last player in the NFL to go "both ways," to play defense and offense. On defense I am a middle linebacker, a perennial all-pro who averages fifteen unassisted tackles a game. On offense I am a tailback, also a perennial all-pro at that position, averaging 150 yards rushing a game. That's it; that's the fantasy. Don't judge me—just think of whatever silly, delusional fantasies you entertain. Of course I was nothing like that as a player. The joke was, "Ben isn't very big, but he's slow." I had the heart of a great athlete, in desire, dedication, and discipline; but I had the body of a pretty average athlete. I was an overachiever; my passion for the sport could take me right up to what my genetic endowment, my DNA, would allow, but no further.

But what if I was given a new DNA, new and extraordinary capacities by God? What if I experienced a kind of second birth athletically and was made fully capable of becoming all I have fantasized? Would that miracle make me lazy? Would knowing what I had the ability to become make me complacent? Of course not—I would strive with everything in me to work out what God had worked in. It would still be hard to be a champion, but it would be a good hard.

The Bible says God has given us everything we need to live a godly life, including such "great and precious promises" that we may actually "share his divine nature." The strenuous life of good works, in fact, is part of our new spiritual DNA. How then should we live? "In view of all this," we should "*make every effort* to respond to God's promises" (2 Peter 1:3-5, italics mine). It is the glory and joy of all believers to "travail" as in the pains of childbirth until Christ is fully developed in their lives.[5]

And O, that He fulfilled may see
The travail of His soul in me,
And with His work contented be,
As I with my dear Savior!

"I AM NOT SKILLED TO UNDERSTAND" BY
DORA GREENWELL (1821–1882)

CHAPTER 2

THE GOD WHO CALLS

GOD IS A WARRIOR

The Lord is a warrior; Yahweh is his name!
EXODUS 15:3

But isn't it true that "God is love"? . . . God is a lover, not a warrior, right?
No, God is a lover who is a warrior.
PETER KREEFT, *HOW TO WIN THE CULTURE WAR*

I'VE REPLAYED THIS conversation in my mind hundreds of times. It took place with a sweet woman in my church after I regaled her with an account of a great sermon I had heard by John Piper. He had preached on spiritual warfare and the necessary conflict and struggle that goes with the Christian walk, the *agon*. He drove his point home with the jarring words, "To live is to fight." When I got to that part of my account and said fervently, "To live is to fight," I saw her eyes narrow and some of the color drain from her face. She interrupted me and said indignantly, "No! To live isn't to *fight*—to live is *Christ*!" It was clear to her that I had exchanged Jesus for war, the God of love for the idol of struggle.

I should not have been surprised, for the statement that so inspired me, and still does, is but the tip of a massive iceberg of biblical theology. Peter Kreeft sums up the iceberg: "But isn't it true that 'God is love' (1 John 4:16)? God is a lover, not a warrior, right? No, God is a lover who is a warrior."[1] If it is true that to live is Christ, then it is also true that to live is to fight, for the Christ we live for is a warrior. God the warrior in no way contradicts God the lover. Parents know this instinctively; like God the Father/Warrior, they know that love fights and rages and wars against love's enemies—hate and deceit and abuse—anything that would hurt the beloved.

To be with God is to be in a fight—it goes with the relationship. But this takes some explaining.

A WARRIOR'S FOOT ON THE NECK OF A FOE

Question: Which psalm is most quoted or alluded to in the New Testament? This isn't a Bible trivia question—it taps into the heart of some of the most sacred and central mysteries of Christian faith. It's not Psalm 23 or 103; it's not "The LORD is my shepherd," or "Praise the LORD, my soul"; and it's definitely not a happy psalm, at least in the immediate sense of happy. It is warlike and bloody, and it speaks exuberantly of the lands of God's enemies being filled with corpses and heads being shattered over the whole earth.

The psalm is Psalm 110, and every statement in the New Testament declaring Jesus to be sitting at the place of supreme authority at the right hand of God comes directly from this psalm, the first line of which reads:

The LORD said to my Lord,
  "Sit in the place of honor at my right hand
until I humble your enemies,
  making them a footstool under your feet."

The spirit and language of this warlike psalm is everywhere in the New Testament.

Item: Most Christians rightly think of Christ's exaltation to God's right hand as an honor, but none that I know have ever thought of it as also the opposite for his enemies, a humiliation the equivalent of a victorious warrior's foot on the neck of a vanquished foe. I certainly never did, until I saw the way the apostle Paul connected Psalm 110 with Jesus' resurrection, declaring that God crushed and shamed his enemies when he raised Jesus from the dead. "For Christ must reign until he *humbles all his enemies beneath his feet.* And the last enemy to be destroyed is death" (1 Corinthians 15:25-26, italics mine).

Love's triumph over death meant death's death and the taunt, "O death, where is your victory? O death, where is your sting?" (1 Corinthians 15:55).

A VIOLENT FULFILLMENT OF A VIOLENT PSALM

Item: In his letter to the Ephesians, Paul quoted Psalm 110, saying that the same power that raised Jesus from the dead is the power that *"seated him in the place of honor at God's right hand* in the heavenly realms . . . far above any ruler or authority or power or leader or anything else—not only in this world but also in the world to come" (Ephesians 1:20-21, italics mine).

In other words, Christ's resurrection and his enthronement are one and the same event, spiritually violent fulfillments of this violent psalm, which describes the impact of God's victory as a disaster for the enemies of God. Its language is shocking; the Messiah is told:

> The LORD will extend your powerful kingdom from
>   Jerusalem;
>   you will rule over your enemies. . . .
> The Lord stands at your right hand to protect you.
>   He will strike down many kings when his anger erupts.
> He will punish the nations
>   and fill their lands with corpses;
>   he will shatter heads over the whole earth. (Psalm
>   110:2, 5-6)

I could go on and on, and I will, because the Bible does.

Item: When God set the Hebrew slaves free from Egyptian bondage, he didn't sneak them out of Egypt, slipping them past their captors under cover of darkness—he smashed their captors, exposing their gods as frauds and drowning their army in the Red Sea. The spontaneous dance and freedom song that broke out in the aftermath was ecstatic:

> Then Moses and the people of Israel sang this song to the
> LORD:

"I will sing to the LORD,
  for he has triumphed gloriously;
he has hurled both horse and rider
  into the sea.
The LORD is my strength and my song;
  he has given me victory.
This is my God, and I will praise him—
  my father's God, and I will exalt him!
The LORD is a warrior;
  Yahweh is his name!" (Exodus 15:1-3)

WHOSE BLOOD IS IT?

The Lord is a warrior? That's right. This theme so pervades Scripture that in his preface to his landmark monograph, *God Is a Warrior,* Tremper Longman remarks, "It is testimony to my prematurely failing memory that I cannot remember what first caught my interest in this theme, but I do recall the wonder that I felt that after so many years of reading the Bible I had never before noticed how pervasive the theme of God's battles was."[2]

Item: We may not have noticed this theme, but the powers of darkness always have. Remember how Christ's birth was greeted by the tyrant Herod's attempt to kill him by ordering the mass murder of all babies near his age? Demoniacs routinely met Jesus with shrieks of terror and the raging plea that he not torture them or throw them into the abyss. Jesus characterized Satan as a fully armed strong man guarding his palace and possessions (not unlike the way Pharaoh guarded the Hebrew slaves) and he himself as a stronger man who "attacks and overpowers him, strips him of his weapons, and carries off his belongings" (Luke 11:22). How many Christians think of Christ's saving work as attacking and overpowering the enemy of our souls, stripping him of his possessions—which would be us!—and carrying the redeemed off to freedom?

Item: One of the last pictures of Christ in the Bible is of a warrior riding a white horse, leading an army, waging "a righteous war" and releasing "the fierce wrath of God, the Almighty, like juice flowing from a winepress" (Revelation 19:11, 15). One of the most striking features of this warrior-king is his robe, which has been dipped in blood. Whose blood? Some commentators say it must be his blood, since the Bible says we are redeemed by Christ's blood. Other commentators think it might be the blood of his enemies, since it is their blood that is shed "like juice flowing from a winepress." I say, do we have to choose? In ancient battles the victor's sword and the vanquished's sword both did their work, and in the end the victor would often stand covered both by his own blood and the blood of his enemy.

PRAY WARRIOR PRAYERS

Item: In Eastern Orthodox theology, the earthquake that followed Christ's death is understood to be the rumblings that came up from the realm of death and hades as Christ went down to set prisoners free. All heaven broke loose in hell, as he literally went down, seized the keys of death, and took over the place. Be that as it may, we do know that when John saw him in his vision on Patmos, Christ announced himself as "the living one. I died, but look—I am alive forever and ever! And I hold the keys of death and the grave" (Revelation 1:18). The thought of him seizing the keys certainly fires my imagination. Did he not say to Peter, "On this rock I will build my church, and the gates of Hades will not overcome it" (Matthew 16:18, NIV), a distinctly military metaphor, literally enacted in his death and resurrection?

Item: Jesus instructed us to pray for God's Kingdom to come, an inherently warlike act. Think of it: In order for God's Kingdom to come, the old kingdom must move over to make room for the new Kingdom, which of course never happens peacefully and always means war. Do we understand how dangerously hostile and aggressive it is to ask God, publicly no less, to come, take names, and take over the place? To pray the way Jesus told us to pray is to align ourselves with the One who intends to humble his enemies and make them a footstool under his feet. Do we realize what we're actually doing—does anybody?—when we rattle off that warlike prayer? Eugene Peterson writes:

> Everybody treats us so nicely. No one seems to think
> that we mean what we say. When we say "kingdom
> of God," no one gets apprehensive, as if we had just

announced (which we thought we had) that a powerful army is poised on the border, ready to invade. When we say radical things like "Christ," "love," "believe," "peace," and "sin"—words that in other times and cultures excited martyrdoms—the sounds enter the stream of conversation with no more splash than baseball scores and grocery prices.[3]

WHAT IS JESUS DOING RIGHT NOW?

All this brings us to the key role Christians are to play in the fight: to pray warrior prayers, just as Jesus is doing right this moment—to pray with him, actually. And while we'll talk more near the end of the book about prayer and why it is so essential in our fight for the faith, we can't consider what Christ is doing even now to usher in his Kingdom without talking about intercessory prayer.

To pray the way Jesus told us to pray is to align ourselves with the One who intends to humble his enemies and make them a footstool under his feet.

There is a cryptic verse in Psalm 110 that the author of Hebrews seizes upon to make that very point:

> *The LORD has taken an oath and will not break his vow:*
> *"You are a priest forever in the order of Melchizedek."*
> (Psalm 110:4)

Melchizedek was a mysterious figure, a priest-king, who appeared seemingly out of nowhere, from heaven, as it were, to bless Abram after he had won an important battle (see Genesis 14:18-20). Quoting this verse from Psalm 110, the inspired author of Hebrews declares Melchizedek to be a prefigurement of Christ, and Christ to be the fulfillment of the priest-king Melchizedek, now living forever in heaven, to bless his people and pray for us. "Therefore he is able, once and forever, to save those who come to God through him. He lives forever to intercede with God on their behalf" (Hebrews 7:25).

The insight the New Testament brings to our understanding of our warrior-God is that ultimately the battle is not "against flesh-and-blood enemies, but against evil rulers and authorities of the unseen world, against mighty powers in this dark world, and against evil spirits in the heavenly places" (Ephesians 6:12). Wars on earth are not the real wars, but dim, ugly reflections of the invisible, cosmic struggle.[4] The New Testament perspective is that there are unseen powers behind the thrones of this world—darker and more malevolent than the darkest powers we know. The likes of Hitler, Stalin, the kingpins of the Colombian drug cartels, and Osama bin Laden are not the real enemies; they are merely slaves, houseboys, and lackeys for the evil powers of darkness in the unseen world. The multibillion-dollar pornography industry, abortionists, and human traffickers serve powers they don't even know about.

And what is Christ doing about our enemies right now?

Surely we don't know everything exactly, but what we do know, what God has chosen to reveal to us, is that he is praying. In fact, as far as I know, that is the only thing the Bible tells us about what he is doing right now.[5] And he calls us to join him in his great work of intercession. What a wonderful and encouraging thought that is! When we pray, we aren't informing Jesus about the raw evil and brokenness of this world because he is already praying about those things. Prayer is not so much communication with Jesus as it is communion with warrior-Jesus in the fight, the *agon*. When we pray, we lock arms with him in spiritual warfare. Prayer is spiritual warfare, or as David Wells puts it, "the ultimate interference with the status quo."

> Prayer is not so much communication with Jesus as it is communion with warrior-Jesus in the fight, the *agon*.

PRAYER: JOB ONE

But are there not warrior deeds to be done too? There are, but prayer is a deed, a mighty deed; like the Cross, it is the foolishness of God that is wiser than human wisdom, the weakness of God that is stronger than human strength.[6] There is more to do than pray, but we won't get to it until we do pray, for as A. J. Gordon warns us, "You can do more than pray after you have prayed, but you can never do more than pray until you have prayed." Prayer is the fundamental act of the Christian warrior, without which nothing else can happen.

God is a warrior. To pray is to fight with him; not to pray is to refuse to fight, to go spiritually AWOL, and to abandon one's post in battle. Prayerlessness is ultimately *apostasy*, from the Greek *apo*, "to abandon," and *stasis*, "post or place." So God compares intercessors to faithful watchmen standing as sentinels at their post on the walls of Jerusalem:

> *O Jerusalem, I have posted watchmen on your walls;*
> *they will pray day and night, continually.*
> *Take no rest, all you who pray to the LORD.*
> *Give the LORD no rest until he completes his work,*
> *until he makes Jerusalem the pride of the earth.*
> (Isaiah 62:6-7)

Pray Until Something Happens

George Orwell certainly was not thinking about spiritual warfare and these watchmen when he wrote, "People sleep peaceably in their beds at night because rough men stand ready to do violence on their behalf."[7] But I have taken that phrase as a watchword for those who watch on the walls and do battle for God. We will never know till eternity what those prayers have meant.

But a look into the eighth chapter of Revelation can help our perspective, for it lifts the veil on what is actually going on in heaven as we pray. In his vision, John saw an angel with a gold incense burner standing at the altar before the throne of God. The smoke rising up from the censer contained the prayers of God's people, mixed with incense from the altar. That alone is a vivid picture of the power of prayer, for prayer is to God what the fragrance and smoke of incense is to our nostrils. The sense of smell is perhaps the most compelling and evocative of all our senses. And what follows is shocking. The angel filled this prayer-censer "with fire from the altar and threw it down upon the earth; and thunder crashed, lightning flashed, and there was a terrible earthquake" (cf. Revelation 8:1-5). In other words, all creation is being shaken by the prayers of God's people!

Think of the prayer meetings you have attended. Have you ever felt the world was being shaken by your prayers? I never have. The truth is, it often seems that the words I speak are doing no more than dribbling down on the carpet, or bouncing off the acoustical tiles on the ceiling of my church's prayer room. The effect of acoustical tile is a good metaphor for how prayer can feel: muffled and impotent.

But we live by unseen realities. The seen world may appear solid and permanent, the unseen ephemeral and insubstantial. Reality is precisely the opposite. It takes imagination to pray—sanctified imagination—for though prayer can seem tame and tempt us to drop off to sleep, prayer is a violent and hateful encounter with the enemies of God, because to pray is to join our wills with the most dangerous figure in the universe: Jesus, the warrior-priest who even now intercedes for us.

CHAPTER 3

DON'T TRY THIS ALONE

FIGHTING AS ONE BODY

Above all, you must live as citizens of heaven, conducting yourselves in a manner worthy of the Good News about Christ. Then, whether I come and see you again or only hear about you, I will know that you are standing together with one spirit and one purpose, fighting together for the faith, which is the Good News.
PHILIPPIANS 1:27

The man who seeks God in isolation from his fellows is likely to find, not God, but the devil, who will bear an embarrassing resemblance to himself.
R. H. TAWNEY

My SOPHOMORE YEAR in high school, the year I signed up to try out for the football team, held a defining moment in my life. I will never forget the excitement and apprehension I felt as I walked into the room where all the other boys were going to meet the coach. There was the smell of liniment and sweat, the sound of metal lockers slamming shut, the hiss of showers, and the sight of all those gigantic seniors.

The head coach of the varsity team had been a drill instructor in the Marine Corps. He had a thick neck and a crew cut, his voice was gravelly from all the shouting he had done in his life, and he had been very successful as a coach.

By the time he appeared, we had been sitting in the room

for a few minutes, doing all the things a bunch of nervous adolescent boys do: laughing extra loud, trying to look cool and confident, and doing everything we could to conceal our terror of the man who was about to walk into the room. In he came, the head coach, followed by an entourage of assistants, trainers, and managers. He slammed his clipboard down on a table, scowled at all of us, and announced that he was going to tell us the three Ds of winning football. They were: dedication, desire, and discipline.

There was absolute silence as he took each of these words and told us what they must mean to all of us if we expected to play football on his team. When he got to the last D, discipline, he explained that it revealed whether or not we were really serious about the first two, desire and dedication; whether they were only warm, cozy feelings with no substance; whether there was any reality to our commitment. To make his point, he told us what had happened the first year he was the varsity coach. Football at our school had been a failure up until the time he arrived, but that first year had promise—there were a number of very talented seniors on the squad. But when these upperclassmen heard his speech about the three Ds, he could tell they all thought it a bit amusing. In particular, he noticed some eye-rolling when he came to the part about discipline, since part of the discipline of playing meant no late nights out during the week and no drinking of alcoholic beverages whatsoever.

The team was three games into the season, and undefeated, when Coach heard that all the seniors had gone to a party and gotten drunk after the third game. He summarily kicked all the seniors off the team and moved up a bunch of sophomores and juniors to fill their positions. After that, they lost the rest of their games and finished the year with three wins and six losses. But the next year Coach had a team with more experience, and a lot more discipline, and they finished second in the conference. And from that year on they were the team to beat.

When he finished his speech, there was at least one young man in that room who knew he meant business and who believed in the three Ds of winning football, especially the third one. I still do.

DISCIPLINE HAS ITS REASONS

Two things impressed me that day: One was the fact that discipline has its reasons. I had always thought of discipline as a masochistic exercise in self-denial, of giving up something simply for the sake of giving it up, as though there was some intrinsic good in deprivation. What I began to understand was that discipline really means giving up something lesser for something greater. Washington Irving wrote, "Great minds have purposes; others have wishes." Discipline is what separates purposes from wishes, great minds from little minds, solid accomplishment from mere dreams.

It didn't take me long to see the connection of discipline

> ✗ Discipline really means giving up something lesser for something greater.

Handwritten margin notes: God - all-knowing knows what's best for me / Am I disciplined enough to realize that & wait for His timing His best for me?

with far more important things than football. In football, the "greater" is success on the playing field. But the stakes are small in the grand scheme of the universe. What about the Kingdom of God? Here the stakes are eternal, the highest. The "greater" goal of the spiritual disciplines is to be formed in the image of Christ, to enjoy nothing less than sharing in God's glory; to receive the "great and precious promises . . . that enable you to share [God's] divine nature and escape the world's corruption caused by human desires" (2 Peter 1:4).

The devil may understand this better than many Christians do. In C. S. Lewis's fantasy *The Screwtape Letters*, the senior demon Screwtape warns his nephew, the junior demon Wormwood, that God is "a hedonist at heart." This disgusts the devil and is evidence to him that in the spiritual disciplines God is really hiding from the humans his real intent, which is to make us happy:

> All those fasts and vigils and stakes and crosses are
> only a façade. Or only like foam on the seashore.
> Out at sea, out in His sea, there is pleasure, and
> more pleasure. He makes no secret of it; at His right
> hand are "pleasures for evermore". Ugh! . . . He's
> vulgar, Wormwood. He has a bourgeois mind. He
> has filled His world full of pleasures.[1]

God calls us to disciplined and orderly lives for our greater good. He has greater plans for us than we could ever have for ourselves. He teaches us to say no to lesser things in order to say yes to great things. His vision of our humanity is such that if we could see now what, by his grace, we will one day be, we would see a creature of such beauty and goodness that we would be strongly tempted to worship.[2]

The second idea was harder to get my mind around—and more important. Discipline, laying down the lesser for the sake of the greater, can be something a team or a community does together. A group of people, united by great purposes and holy passion and held together by a rigorous common discipline, will be more than the sum of its parts.

The saying "United we stand, divided we fall" is more than a slogan; it is empirically verifiable. Following my coach's speech, I was to learn

> A group of people, united by great purposes and holy passion and held together by a rigorous common discipline, will be more than the sum of its parts.

from experience that the success of my high school football team could be sabotaged by just a few slackers—and was, in fact, more than once. It has been more than fifty years, but I can still feel the resentment rising in my throat when I remember the times so many of us worked so very hard and our efforts were neutralized by just a few undisciplined louts. My senior year we lost a game that effectively put us out of contention for the league championship because our starting quarterback and star fullback got kicked out of the game for punching players on the other team.

NO CHRISTIAN IS AN ONLY CHILD

Hall of Fame quarterback Steve Young said football is chore-ography. It's like a dance that involves a variety of people with diverse skills and body types—in what other sport could elephantine fat men play with lithe gazelles?—and requires that each does his part in concert with all the others. If the football analogy doesn't speak to you, think of the beauty that emerges from a symphony orchestra, when many sounds and parts unite as one.

My introduction to what it meant to be on a football team set me up to begin to understand something much more important than football—the church. The church is the body of Christ, with each and every individual Christian a member, organically connected to the whole. For the Christian, it can never be simply a matter of "me and God." It is always "we and God." It's like this: Whenever Christ sees a crowd of people he does two things. First he disperses it and isolates each and every person, one-on-one, in per-sonal encounter with himself. The second thing he does is to reintroduce all those isolated individuals to each other as members, no longer of a crowd, but of a body—his body, the church. Those two things are connected in such a way that to deny one is to deny the other.

This being the case, to fight the good fight and finish the race cannot be something a Christian does merely as an individual. Individual Christians must do their part, as those who participate in a dance or a concert or a football

game—but always as a part of something bigger. This is hard
to swallow for many individualistic American Christians, but
it is essential to following Jesus. Remember when Peter confessed his individual faith to Jesus? "You are the Messiah,
the Son of the living God." Jesus responded to Peter's faith
by making Peter a church member! He said, "You are Peter
(which means 'rock'), and upon this rock I will build my
church" (Matthew 16:16, 18).

We think Jesus came to save souls, one soul at a time,
which is right, as far as it goes; but it doesn't go far enough,
for he saves souls in the community of all the other souls he is
saving. The community is part of the saving. When someone
complains that the church is full of hypocrites and that they
want no part of it, I say, "Then you should be very comfortable in the church. You'll find a lot of people just like you,
who are being saved from their hypocrisy, just like you, too,
will be saved from yours." ☺ Amen!

The writer to the Hebrews urges us to "run with endurance the race God has set before us . . . keeping our eyes
on Jesus, the champion who initiates and perfects our faith"
(Hebrews 12:1-2). But as we run, our eyes on Jesus, he also
says there are many eyes on us: all those believers who have
gone before us, "a huge crowd of witnesses" whose heroic
lives were described in the previous chapter of Hebrews. I've
long imagined these folks—people like Noah, Abraham,
Sarah, Moses, Rahab, and David—as sitting up in the stands
resting, having successfully run their race, and now watching
us run ours, cheering us on to do as well as they did. It has

essentially been a picture of individuals watching other individuals run, urging them to do their best. But the Scripture says something more profound and more corporate is going on in those heavenly stands, for "none of them received all that God had promised. For God had something better in mind for us, so that they would not reach perfection without us" (Hebrews 11:39-40).

TOGETHER OR NOT AT ALL

These heroes of the faith are not done till we are done, and we're not done till those who come after us are done! They will not reach perfection until we have, and we will not reach perfection until all whom God has called into his church have reached perfection. We fight the good fight together, or not at all, for we are the body of Christ—not the assembly, or the association, or the society, but the body of Christ.

Philosopher Peter Kreeft calls this "the great principle of solidarity, spiritual and mystical and universal." Individuals matter to God; he has even numbered the hairs on our heads. But individuals cease to be individuals the moment they are torn out of the body, the way an eye would cease to be an eye the moment it was removed from a head and put on a saucer. It no longer sees outside the body—and the rest of the body suffers because it no longer sees. The warrior ceases to be a warrior the moment the warrior is removed from the body. Worse, removed from the body, the individualistic warrior is not merely neutralized but begins to fight for the enemy."

"Every sin harms everyone in the Body, and every act of love and obedience to the Head helps every organ in the Body," writes Kreeft. The principle is built into the very structure of the created order:

> Even the physical universe works this way. Gravity is universal. Every particle of matter in the universe "loves" and gravitationally affects every other particle of matter in the universe, and we can calculate exactly how much if we only know their mass and distance. How much more must there be a universal spiritual gravity.
>
> When you . . . say a loving and helpful word to your family, some martyr three thousand miles and three hundred years away may receive enough grace to endure his trials because of you. And if instead you sin one more time this afternoon, that martyr may weaken, compromise and be broken. If there is a universal spiritual gravity, if we all help or harm each other, there must be some one straw that breaks the camel's back, one vote that decides the election. *Everything matters.* There are no "victimless crimes." Every sin against Christ harms his Body and every member in it.[3] ~ not some, or a few or a certain few but All

If this is a new idea to you, consider this: The sin of Achan dramatically affected the whole nation of Israel (see Joshua 7:1). Should I say more? The risen Christ told the seven

35

churches to deal with sin in the community or he would remove their candlesticks. Paul warned the Corinthians that a little yeast leavens the whole lump (see 1 Corinthians 5:6). On the positive side, Paul held up the generosity of a poor church in Macedonia, to stimulate the generosity of a rich church in Corinth. He later explained how every act of love and generosity is like sowing seed in soil; the impact of the seed far exceeds its size because of its connection to the soil (2 Corinthians 8:1-8; 9:6-10). This holds true even in our relationship to the world. Jesus said we are the salt of the earth, and everyone knows it doesn't take a lot of salt to alter the flavor of food.

THE GREATEST ARGUMENT

No wonder that on the night before he went to the Cross, our Lord Jesus prayed that we would be one, just as he and his Father are one. And he attributed to that oneness a power he attributes to nothing else: it will convince the world that he came from God and that God loves his church as much as he loves his Son: "I am in

The greatest argument for the reality of Christ comes from the simplest Christians who live together in the unity of the Spirit in the body of Christ.

them and you are in me. May they experience such perfect unity that the world will know that you sent me and that you love them as much as you love me" (John 17:23).

Amazing! The greatest argument for the reality of Christ

Reality of Christ

does not come from philosophers and theologians. It comes from the simplest Christians who live together in the unity of the Spirit in the body of Christ.

Why does unity have this kind of power? Because when we live together in love and harmony, it can mean but one thing: that each of us has ceased being our own lord and has submitted to the real Lord. This is hugely significant, for when we submit to the lordship of Christ there can no longer be room for isolated individualism, the attitude that Archbishop William Temple criticized when he said, tongue in cheek, "I believe in one holy, infallible church, of which I regret to say that at the present time I am the only member." The economist R. H. Tawney was speaking in the same tone when he wrote, "The man who seeks God in isolation from his fellows is likely to find, not God, but the devil, who will bear an embarrassing resemblance to himself."[4] When Christ is truly Lord over his own people, his power is released and radiates out into the world, because the church begins to look like the God who is himself a community of love—Father, Son, and Holy Spirit. *// T you Jesus*

No wonder then that the writer to the Hebrews gave such significance to meeting together for the express purpose of mutually urging each other on to love and obedience. He uses a word that is used elsewhere in the Bible in a negative sense, as in spurring or provoking someone to anger. But here it is to provoke to love: "And let us consider how we may spur one another on toward love and good deeds" (Hebrews 10:24, NIV). A pastor quoted this verse to me when

love w/ Jesus eyes

I was in college, and added, "You know, Ben, every Christian has the right—no, the responsibility—to expect obedience to God from every other Christian." At first I was offended at what he said, but he was right. My business is never just my business only. It's yours, too. If we belong to Christ, we belong to each other. The worst thing a soldier can do to a fellow soldier in a battle is to become lazy and inattentive or cowardly. One man's lapse can mean another man's death. So Paul instructed the Philippians to conduct themselves in a manner worthy of the Good News about Christ, "standing together with one spirit and one purpose, fighting together for the faith, which is the Good News" (Philippians 1:27).

How good it is when Christians voluntarily enter into relationship with each other for the stated purpose of encouraging each other to live holy lives. And how hard it can be—but a good hard! I could write my spiritual autobiography by the names of the men and women who have loved me enough to call me to holy living and who have trusted me enough to call them to do the same.

DELIVER US FROM ME-VILLE

Jesus taught us to pray, "Deliver us from evil." That's a good prayer for a warrior to pray. And as David Zimmerman put it in his marvelous little book, in order to be delivered from evil, we should also pray, "Deliver us from me-ville."[5] It's foolish to fight the good fight alone—impossible, really. And it's often fatal, spiritually. In solitude, a believer is vulnerable, like the baby wildebeest I saw in the Masai Mara game reserve in southwestern Kenya. Somehow he had been separated from the herd and was following our Land Rover in the hope, it seemed, that we could be some kind of surrogate mother.

The wildebeest is an antelope-like creature, its name coming from the Dutch, meaning "wild cattle." Cattle, like sheep, are defenseless outside the herd, or flock. As he trotted behind us, bleating plaintively, we looked around hoping to find a herd of his own kind that perhaps we could lead him to. The plain was filled with predators, and we knew he'd be lucky if he wasn't gobbled up by some creature before nightfall. At one point he saw a mother rhinoceros with her young and tried them out for companionship. But the mother drove him away, and he ran back to us.

Moments later we drove around a bend near the river, right into the middle of a pack of hyenas sunning themselves. We all wanted to shoo the baby away from what we had led him into, but there was no way; and the only humor in the situation was the surprised delight on the hyenas' faces as they saw an afternoon snack walk right into their midst. Several jumped up, circled the youngster, and tore him to pieces in seconds. He hardly had time to cry out. It wasn't our fault, of course, but we all still felt responsible for his death. But the truth is a wildebeest, alone on the African plain, cannot exist apart from the herd. It's dangerous out there, outside the protection of the herd.

Likewise, there are hyenas who would like nothing better than to eat you. We know, do we not, that here is the devil,

Dangerous when we are not protected by the Father's hands

who the Bible says prowls around like a roaring lion seeking whom he may devour (see 1 Peter 5:8)? The classic theological categories include not only the devil, but also the world and our own sinful nature. These enemies of our souls never stop attacking us. We cannot fight pride, lust, avarice, gluttony, unbelief, and sloth alone. No one is strong enough and alert enough for that. We need Christ to survive, and he has chosen to give us his strength through his body, the church. It is our fault if we separate ourselves from Christ's body. Me-Ville is the sin that makes us prey to every other kind of evil, the pride beneath all sin.

The Heart is desperately wicked who can know it!

PART 2

THE CASE FOR A VIGOROUS FAITH

WHY DOES JESUS SPEAK WITH SUCH SEVERITY AND URGENCY?

I BEGAN MY JOURNEY of faith as a ten-year-old in a neighborhood Good News Club, an outreach of Child Evangelism Fellowship. You might say I am a product of "popsicle evangelism," since Mrs. Dalton, the dear lady who led me to Christ, enticed us to come to the meetings in her home with the promise of free popsicles.

But she kept us coming back by telling us stories from the Bible's greatest hits: Noah and the Flood, Samson and the Philistines (she left the R-rated Delilah part out), David and Goliath, and the like. But no matter what the story was, she ended with an invitation to let Jesus come into our hearts. She would show us a picture of a big red heart. In the center of the paper heart was a picture of Jesus knocking on a door. She would point out that the door had no knob on the outside, that the only knob was on the inside, and that the only way Jesus could come in was if we ourselves opened the door and let him in. Then she would quote Revelation 3:20 from the King James Version: "Behold, I stand at the door, and knock: if any man hear my voice, and open the door, I will come in to him, and will sup with him, and he with me."

She said that if we let Jesus in, he would come in and sup with us and live in our hearts. Then, when we died, we would live with him in heaven forever. The alternative to living with Christ forever was to live in hell forever, and though I was a little hazy about the "sup" part, I was crystal clear about the hell part. I thought, *Such a deal! Who could pass this up?* I opened the door to my heart, and as primitive as my theology was, I believe I became a child of God that day. It was Ben plus Jesus equals heaven. After years of graduate school in theology and decades of being a pastor, the kernel of my faith has remained intact.

But there was very little I understood about Ben or Jesus back then. All I could do was give what I knew of myself to what I knew of him—which is all any of us can ever do. In fact, I think a good one-line definition of the Christian faith is giving what you know of yourself to what you know of God. Authentic faith is dynamic; it's not a fixed quantity because to know Christ is to be ever growing in the knowing—of yourself and of him. Since the day I let Jesus come into my heart, my knowledge of myself and of Jesus has been expanding—not in a neat, orderly progression from one degree of glory to another, but in fits and starts, periods of peace and quiet and stagnation, interrupted by conflict and anguish and joy, glorious and inexpressible.

And Jesus can be a difficult housemate. For one thing, he is a warrior. For another, he always brings his friends in with him, some of whom I don't like. He calls them his church. And he insists that the road is hard, very hard. But I picture him smiling as he says it, and he calls it a good hard, a good fight, something not to be missed for all the world.

So there has been a lot to learn about Ben and Jesus—especially Jesus. That's where the "supping" part comes in. The New Living Translation renders that word "share a meal together as friends." The idea is that life with Jesus, though demanding, is meant to be a communion, a fellowship of friends in which he takes us into his confidence and teaches us to see the world as he sees the world, to think as he thinks. It's in that communion that he makes his case for a vigorous faith and we begin to understand why he speaks with such severity and urgency.

CHAPTER 4

THE WAR

DON'T TAKE IT PERSONALLY

Whatever others may do in religion the Lord Jesus would have us know that our duty is clear. The gate is straight. The work is great. The enemies of our souls are many. We must be up and doing. We are to wait for nobody. We are not to inquire what other people are doing, and whether many of our neighbors and friends are serving Christ. The unbelief and indecision of others will be no excuse on that last day. We must never follow a multitude to do evil. If we go to heaven alone we must resolve that by God's grace we will go. Whether we have many with us or a few, the command before us is plain—"strive to enter in."
J. C. RYLE, *EXPOSITORY THOUGHTS ON THE GOSPELS*

For we are not fighting against flesh-and-blood enemies, but against evil rulers and authorities of the unseen world, against mighty powers in this dark world, and against evil spirits in the heavenly places.
EPHESIANS 6:12

War is not something that illustrates aspects of Christian living. Christian living is war. Indeed, I would go further. Earthly warfare is not the real warfare. It is but a faint, ugly reflection of the real thing. It is into the *real* war that the Christian is to plunge.
JOHN WHITE, *THE FIGHT*

IF GOD IS a warrior, then there must be a war.

The Bible says there is, but you don't have to believe the Bible to know that it is true. It's hard to miss. Who can look at the blood-splattered face of human history and not see that there is a terror and rage that stalks and claws and tears away at the earth and its peoples? It has always been this way. Take the twentieth century, for instance; the greatest killer was not war, actually—nations killing other nations. The greatest killer was nations killing their own people, governments killing the governed. Cautious estimates have nearly 80 million people murdered in the twentieth century—killed systematically and with scientific precision sometimes, by their own rulers. Hitler's killing of 6 million Jews is well documented. And this by a nation many considered to be the best educated and most cultured in all Europe. Not so well known are the nearly 40 million people Stalin killed, including 7 million Ukrainians during a forced famine. The Armenians and Cambodians have their own stories of horror, as do the Chinese, the Ugandans, the Ethiopians, and the people of Rwanda, Darfur, and the Congo.

TOO BIG, TOO DEEP, TOO PERVASIVE

The war isn't just out there; it's next door, and it boils in families and neighborhoods. A friend of mine, a police chief, told me of a family on the east side of his town that he regularly visited in his days as a patrolman, before he became a chief. His many calls to this family were always domestic violence disputes, so many that he was on a first-name basis with everybody in the family. It was always the same: There would be a drunk, cursing husband; a battered and cowering wife; and several terrified children huddled in a corner. My friend would handcuff the husband, book him, and release him within a few hours because his wife would never press charges. The sad, brutal cycle went on for years.

Then one evening my friend was called to intervene in a domestic violence episode involving another, younger family in an apartment on the west side of town. The scene was dreary and typical: the pervasive stench of alcohol; a man, drunk and raging; a cringing wife, bruised and bleeding; and children, shivering and sobbing.

He cuffed the belligerent young man, and as he walked him out to his patrol car, the young man asked him, "Do you remember me?"

He looked more closely at the man and saw a glimmer of something familiar, but he couldn't remember where or when. "Your face looks like somebody I once met," he replied, "but I don't remember who."

"You used to arrest my old man out on the east side of town when I was a boy," the young man answered. He then told my friend how his father had advised him to handle things if his "old lady gets out of line," which is what he'd just done.

He was one of the children who used to watch my friend arrest his dad! As my friend helped the young man into the backseat of his patrol car, he looked back at the open door of the apartment where the arrest had been made. There stood another little boy watching his daddy get arrested for beating up his mom. Another generation, another cycle of brutality and confusion, was poised and waiting in that doorway.

Things like this are too big, too deep, too pervasive and

intractable to be explained by the social sciences. G. K. Chesterton was surely right when he said the doctrine of original sin is the only Christian doctrine that is empirically

G. K. Chesterton was surely right when he said the doctrine of original sin is the only Christian doctrine that is empirically verifiable.

verifiable. It's not so much a matter of faith as hard fact.

The hard fact is that we are at war. But the Bible says the real war is not against things accessible to our five senses—the things we can taste, touch, hear, smell, and see. It is "against evil rulers and authorities of the unseen world, against mighty powers in this dark world, and against evil spirits in the heavenly places" (Ephesians 6:12).

SECULARIZATION

The real war is spiritual and cosmic. It's much bigger and scarier than Nazism and Marxism and racism; it's uglier and more degrading than HIV/AIDS, addiction, genocide, pornography, and domestic violence. These things are symptoms, not causes. Biblical cosmology says there is one reality, but with two dimensions—one seen, the other unseen. God made them both, and as the Nicene Creed sums it up, God the Father is "the Almighty maker of heaven and earth, of all that is seen and unseen."

But it is the realm of the unseen that is the larger and more determinative of the two. Though no less real, the seen is an arena in which unseen realities are being acted out. In the words of John White, wars fought in the seen are but "faint, ugly" reflections of the real war in the unseen, mere "tremors felt from an earthquake light-years away. The Christian's war takes place at the epicenter of the earthquake. It is infinitely more deadly, while the issues that hang on it make earth's most momentous questions no more than village gossip."[1]

The reality of this spiritual, cosmic struggle is hard for us to get our minds around, much less believe, because we have been conditioned by a culture that is thoroughly secularized. Secularism is a worldview that limits "official reality" to the five senses, to material things, and asserts that all that happens in this world occurs within a closed system of cause and effect. Secularism is a suffocatingly claustrophobic philosophy; it is, as sociologist Peter Berger put it, a "world without windows."[2] Chesterton's view is more humorous; he said secularism does to the human spirit and imagination what a big, carbohydrate-heavy, four-martini lunch does to middle-aged businessmen—it puts us to sleep, spiritually.

Of course secularism is antithetical to Christianity. But one need not be a secularist to be secular*ized*. Secularism is a philosophy that describes what is real; secularization is a sociological phenomenon that determines what matters, what we do or don't pay attention to. Os Guinness defines secularization as a process by which religious ideas and institutions, practices and interpretations lose their practical social significance. "Practical social significance" is the operative phrase: secularized minds need not deny the reality of the supernatural in order to act as though they didn't think it exists. They simply don't see it as making much difference in practical matters, in the things we do in the world in the realm of the seen. The spiritual is restricted to personal and subjective matters.

Prayer, for instance, can build intimacy in a small group, or calm anxiety, but doesn't really get anything done in the world. Prayer can focus one's mind, but it probably won't pay the rent or end human trafficking. Secularized Christians aren't likely to say this out loud or to formally deny the reality of radical, spiritual evil in the world—they just act as though they do. For the secularized Christian, spiritual warfare is more of a subjective mental construct, or a metaphor for psychosocial dissonances, than the objective, burning reality Scripture insists it is.

> Secularized Christians aren't likely to formally deny the reality of radical, spiritual evil in the world—they just act as though they do.

Like it or not, we are in a war, engaged in an objective, violent spiritual conflict. Do you know just how close to the heart of the gospel this warfare is? It's not on the edge or sequestered in some arcane theological department—it's right in the center. The eminent New Testament scholar N. T. Wright sees it from the beginning, in the Christmas story amid the shepherds and angels and manger:

> Christmas is not about the living God coming to tell us everything's all right. John's gospel isn't about Jesus speaking the truth and everyone saying:

"Of course! Why didn't we realize it before?" It is about God shining his clear, bright torch into the darkness of our world, our lives, our hearts, our imaginations—and the darkness not comprehending it. It's about God, God as a little child, speaking words of truth, and nobody knowing what he's talking about.[3]

On Christmas morning as "the little Lord Jesus lay down his sweet head" and "the stars in the sky looked down where he lay,"[4] the devil sought to devour him. The cattle may have been lowing, but the predator roared. One of his servants, Herod, gave the order to slaughter all the little baby boys in the region where Jesus was born, in the hope that he might be among them. From his very birth, murderous hatred greeted Jesus—and continues to greet all who belong to him. When he grew up, Jesus told his followers, "If they beat on me, they will certainly beat on you" (John 15:20, *The Message*).

I blush to think of how often I have reacted to hardship as though the whole struggle was about me; about my strengths and weaknesses, my character and wisdom—*my feelings*. I've wondered if maybe I should find another line of work, one I'm better at than ministry. I have been quick to define conflict as people making me feel bad.[5] What I need is to get over myself and my preoccupation with how I am experiencing things. It's not about me—it never has been! I belong to Jesus, the Suffering Servant. I shouldn't be hurt and disappointed when the work is hard; I should expect the hardness, even embrace and celebrate it as Jesus said (Matthew 5:11-12) because it's a good hard—it is a fellowship, a communion with the One who said, "If they beat on me, they will certainly beat on you."

The early Puritans understood this. As James I. Packer writes, they knew that "ease and luxury, such as our affluence brings us today, do not make for maturity; hardship and struggle however do. . . . They accepted conflict as their calling, seeing themselves as their Lord's soldier-pilgrims . . . and not expecting to be able to advance a single step without opposition of one sort or another."[6]

For most of my life with Christ I had expected that if I did things right, there would be no conflict. I had assumed that if things got hard it must be because I was doing something wrong. But it might mean the opposite; it might mean that I was doing something right, that I was advancing into enemy territory. And even if I was suffering because I was doing things badly, it was only because my heart and character are part of the enemy territory to be conquered. Either way, it's not about me but about Christ and his Kingdom. To live is to fight.

"WE'RE SUPPOSED TO BE SURROUNDED"

The brilliant HBO miniseries *Band of Brothers* follows a company of US paratroopers through their basic training to the invasion of Europe on D-Day and beyond. Based on the real-life experiences of survivors, whose testimonies are sprinkled throughout the story, the series vividly captures the heroism and suffering of men at war. The dominant character is Lieutenant Richard Winters, a true leader who grasps his calling the way a Christian should grasp his or her calling to conflict. In one scene, after he has led his troops in a charge into battle, Winters is shown saluting an officer he has just promoted and then commenting to another soldier, "I don't like to retreat."

His best line comes as he leads his troops into their finest moment, their stand against the Germans in the Battle of the Bulge. Overwhelmingly outnumbered, he is warned by a soldier leaving the front lines, who pulls him aside and says, "Looks like you guys are going to be surrounded."

Without blinking, Winters answers, "We're paratroopers, Lieutenant. We're supposed to be surrounded."

We should live our lives with that same attitude: We're Christians; we're supposed to contend and struggle in the good fight. If they beat on our Master, they'll beat on us— it's a privilege to be beat on! Our prayer should never be to be taken out of the fight but to embrace and celebrate the fight, for it is a fellowship, a communion with our Master and Commander. He takes delight in his people and calls it a "glorious privilege" to fight with him, his praise in our mouths and a "sharp sword" in our hands:

> *Let the praises of God be in their mouths,*
> *and a sharp sword in their hands—*

to execute vengeance on the nations
  and punishment on the peoples,
to bind their kings with shackles
  and their leaders with iron chains,
to execute the judgment written against them.
  This is the glorious privilege of his faithful ones.

Praise the LORD! (Psalm 149:6-9)

CHAPTER 5

THE STAKES

HEAVEN OR HELL

And what do you benefit if you gain the whole world but lose your own soul?
Is anything worth more than your soul?
JESUS, IN MARK 8:36-37

It ought to be the business of every day to prepare for our last day.
MATTHEW HENRY

IT'S HARD TO follow Jesus. He said, "If you try to hang on to your life, you will lose it. But if you give up your life for my sake and for the sake of the Good News, you will save it" (Mark 8:35). It's hard to follow Jesus, but it's a good hard. To follow Jesus is to choose life over death, heaven over hell, forever. The road to life is a good hard. The road to hell is easy, but it ends in a very, very bad hard: "You can enter God's Kingdom only through the narrow gate. The highway to hell is broad, and its gate is wide for the many who choose that way. But the gateway to life is very narrow and the road is difficult, and only a few ever find it" (Matthew 7:13-14).

Fyodor Dostoyevsky understood this. On December 22, 1849, he stood shivering before a firing squad, tied to a post and robed in a white burial shroud. He and a few others had been convicted of treason by Tsar Nicholas I, who wanted to impress upon other intellectuals the gravity of promoting radical political views. But the execution was staged. At the last minute, as rifles were cocked and raised, and the order, "Ready, aim!" was shouted, a horseman galloped dramatically into the scene with a note from the tsar in hand. Nicholas had mercifully commuted their sentences to four years of hard labor.

BIRTH ASTRIDE A GRAVE

It might have been Dostoyevsky who said the prospect of standing before a firing squad marvelously focuses one's mind. The experience certainly focused his mind and marked him for the rest of his life. His encounter with death made life precious beyond measure. The man who would one day author the incomparable *Crime and Punishment* and *The Brothers Karamazov* said, "Now my life will change; I shall be born again in a new form." God had given him a second chance. Now he was focused on the things that matter.

Focused on the things that matter. We all will face death, whether before a firing squad at age twenty or in a hospice bed at ninety. The mortality rate among humans is 100 percent. "We give birth astride a grave," wrote Samuel Beckett.[1] The inevitability of that prospect—and what comes after—should get our full attention, should marvelously focus the mind. But it often doesn't, because the thought of death is unpleasant. What Blaise Pascal saw among his contemporaries in seventeenth-century France can easily be said of our

times: "Being unable to cure death, wretchedness and ignorance, men have decided, in order to be happy, not to think
about such things."[2]

But refusing to think about unhappy things won't make
them go away. "We do not make the universe hold its breath
by holding ours."[3] Reality doesn't adjust itself to fit our likes
and dislikes. It is tragic foolishness, criminal negligence, not
to make the fact of death a fact of life. As Pascal put it, when
we ignore the reality of death, "we run heedlessly into the
abyss after putting something in front of us to stop us [from]
seeing it."[4] So Pascal tried to shock people into looking where
they were running. He wrote,

God doesn't either

> Imagine a number of men in chains, all under
> sentence of death, some of whom are each day
> butchered in the sight of the others; those remaining
> see their own condition in that of their fellows, and
> looking at each other with grief and despair await
> their turn. This is an image of the human condition.[5]

THE FOUR FINAL THINGS

The great question of life is really a question about death:
How then should one live, knowing that life will end? If
death means nothing more than extinction, then what we
do in life doesn't mean anything. It's just, "Let's feast and
drink, for tomorrow we die!" (1 Corinthians 15:32). But if
there is a reckoning after death—a tribunal to stand before,

a judge to answer to—then everything changes. The Holy Scriptures assert that this is precisely the case, that in the end there are four final things: death, judgment, heaven, and hell. The first two are inevitable, unavoidable. We cannot

It is tragic foolishness, criminal negligence, not to make the fact of death a fact of life.

choose whether to face death and judgment, for we are all "destined to die once, and after that to face judgment" (Hebrews 9:27, NIV).

But we do have a choice about the second two, heaven and hell. All eternity hinges on the choices we make in this life. Martin Luther said there were only two days on his calendar: "today" and "that day." Each second that passes brings us closer to Judgment Day, to "that day." So Matthew Henry believed that "it ought to be the business of every day to prepare for our last day." And Jonathan Edwards resolved "never to do anything I would be afraid to do if it were the last hour of my life."[6]

That's why Jesus said what he did when he was asked if very many were going to be saved. A question about salvation is a question about the four final things—life or death, heaven or hell. So he used an athletic metaphor: he said we should attack the all-important question of salvation the way a runner runs a race or a fighter fights a fight. "Work hard to enter the narrow door to God's Kingdom, for many will try to enter but will fail" (Luke 13:24).

As we have seen, the Greek word translated "work hard," *agon*, was the word used for vigorous athletic competition. It was a fiercely earnest word, applied often to contact sports like boxing and wrestling. It was even used to describe the exertion of a soldier in battle.

Athletes instinctively understand the total attention required by *agon* because they understand judgment. The two, *agon* and judgment, go together because every contest, every competi-

> **Agon and judgment go together because every contest, every competition, has a definite beginning and end, a winner and a loser.**

tion, has a definite beginning and end, with a conclusion, a denouement, a decision; a winner and a loser, or losers. It is the anticipated judgment—the stakes, the numbers on the scoreboard—that marvelously focus the athlete's mind.

THE HARD PART IS GETTING THEM LOST

Jesus said to enter his Kingdom like an athlete, with the same singular focus, because the stakes are the highest. One's life can end in a victory that is inexpressibly and infinitely won- *describe heaven* derful, the anticipation of which is cause for "glorious, inexpressible joy" (1 Peter 1:8). Or one's life can end in a defeat *describe hell* and shame that is unspeakably and infinitely awful, full of "weeping and gnashing of teeth" (Luke 13:28). T. S. Eliot's famous lines about the hollow men, whose lives end not with a bang but a whimper, are true only in the penultimate sense. *pi - next to last* Ultimately, all lives end with a bang. It will be either the roaring joy and exultation of a good fight fought and a race well run, rewarded by God with the crown of life, or it will be the crashing grief and failure of a life wasted.

The words of Jesus about weeping and gnashing of teeth grate on modern sensitivities. Henry David Thoreau was asked if he intended to make peace with God before he died. The question puzzled him. "I did not know that we had ever quarreled,"[7] he blithely replied. In this respect, Thoreau was the quintessential modern.

An evangelist quipped that the hard part about evangelism these days is not getting people saved but getting them lost. C. S. Lewis concurred. He said the greatest barrier he faced in convincing people of their need for Christ was not ignorance but "the almost total absence from the minds of my audience of any sense of sin" and therefore any fear of judgment after death. He regarded this as a relatively new phenomenon in history:

> The early Christian preachers could assume in their hearers . . . a sense of guilt. . . . Thus the Christian message was in those days unmistakably the *Evangelium*, the Good News. It promised healing to those who knew they were sick. We have to convince our hearers of the unwelcome diagnosis before we can expect them to welcome the news of the remedy.

The reason for this change is that, to the modern mind, God and mortals have switched positions:

> The ancient man approached God . . . as the accused person approaches his judge. For the modern man

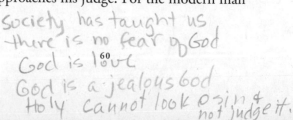

the roles are reversed. He is the judge: God is in the
dock. He is quite a kindly judge: if God should have
a reasonable defense for being the god who permits
war, poverty and disease, he is ready to listen to it.
The trial may even end in God's acquittal. But the
important thing is that Man is on the Bench and
God in the Dock.[8]

But on "that day," on Judgment Day, the only thing that
will matter will be what God thinks of us, not what we think
of God. On "that day" there will be but one relevant question, and it won't be what you thought about the way God
ran the universe. It will be: what did you do with God's offer
of forgiveness and salvation in his Son?

THE GARBAGE DUMP OF ETERNITY

At the heart of the very sweet and tender gospel of God's love
for sinners is a very hard and bitter choice: be loved or be
damned. The alternative to the good news is the possibility
of very, very bad news: death. You may live forever a life that
will be forever marvelous, or you may perish. Take your pick.
"For God loved the world so much that he gave his one and
only Son, so that everyone who believes in him will not *perish*
but have eternal life" (John 3:16, italics mine). It's your call.
Eternal happiness is your choice. But beware; Jeremy Taylor's
words apply here: "God threatens terrible things if we will
not be happy."[9]

Christianity is a rescue religion. Christ is a Savior. Saviors save. We don't need some good advice on how to get on in life, the way people who already know how to swim need tips on how to improve their backstroke. We need to be saved the way a drowning person, a nonswimmer, fallen overboard in an Atlantic storm, needs to be snatched out of the water. We don't need tips; we need salvation. And Jesus said we must grab hold of salvation with *agon*, the same vehement despera- tion with which a drowning person seizes a life preserver. He said to be ruthless with anything that comes between you and salvation, even your most valued possessions, even an eye or a hand:

> *So if your eye—even your good eye—causes you to lust, gouge it out and throw it away. It is better for you to lose one part of your body than for your whole body to be thrown into hell. And if your hand—even your stronger hand—causes you to sin, cut it off and throw it away. It is better for you to lose one part of your body than for your whole body to be thrown into hell.* (Matthew 5:29-30)

When Jesus spoke of hell, he used the word *Gehenna*, the name of the miserable, fetid valley outside Jerusalem where the Jews burned their garbage. Most English translations render the word "hell." Centuries before, it had been the place where the Canaanites performed their diabolic rituals of child sacri- fice and "sacred" prostitution. After the cancer of Canaanite religion was excised from the Promised Land, no Jew would dare to live in that accursed valley. But it could be seen and smelled if one got close enough, for the fires there burned continually, day and night, amid smoldering garbage. No wonder Jesus said it's better to lose a hand or an eye than for your whole body to be thrown into that place, forever.

Jesus said we must grab hold of salvation with *agon*, the same vehement desperation with which a drowning person seizes a life preserver.

How to imagine "forever"? The imagination gets dizzy and light-headed trying. But try this: A bird flies slowly across the universe, from one far edge to the other, traversing distances that can only be measured in light-years. When it reaches the far edge, trillions of miles and days later, it approaches a planet the size of the earth, made of solid diamond. It slowly flies around the planet, and as it does its wing lightly brushes the planet's surface, just once. Then it heads back to where it started, just as slowly and deliberately, again crossing incalculable distances until it reaches the spot where it began. Then it heads back to the diamond planet, slowly, slowly, slowly, until it reaches it, eons later. Again it flies around the planet, and its wing brushes the planet lightly, a second time, just once; and it heads back again to where it began. Okay, okay, I'll stop. But note: The time it will take the bird to wear down the diamond planet to nothing will be but the first second of eternity.

True, the idea of eternity is far richer and more complex than the mere passage of time, measured in amounts. But I

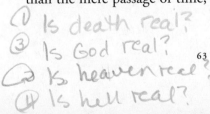

① Is death real?
③ Is God real?
② Is heaven real?
④ Is hell real?

use this illustration to try to convey something of the awful enormity of the loss of being consigned to existence without God and without hope, on and on and on forever in the garbage dump of eternity.

THERE ARE NO ORDINARY PEOPLE

The stakes are the highest. They are matters of life or death, forever. So engage in the *agon*, fight the good fight, run the race, seize the passing moment of your life with vigor and passion—and go after life, go after God, with everything in you. It is the most rational of acts. How could anyone do otherwise? How could anyone run heedlessly into the abyss, deliberately looking the other way? "What do you benefit if you gain the whole world but lose your own soul? Is anything worth more than your soul?" (Mark 8:36-37).

It is crazy the attention modern American Christians give to diet and exercise—to do what? Live longer? How much longer? When set next to eternity, the longest life, even Methuselah's, is a drop in the bucket. There's nothing wrong with proper attention given to diet and exercise, if for no other reasons than that God calls us to be stewards of his creation, and we'll feel better if we do. Caring for the body can be a way of loving God. But Paul warns us that whatever value physical exercise may have, it is far outweighed by spiritual exercise (1 Timothy 4:8). The example of the elite—or not so elite!—athlete makes his point even more compelling. Athletes will devote hours a day of rigorous training for years to win a crown or a medal or even a place on a team; or a musician to play in an orchestra or perform before an audience. All these accolades and accomplishments will fade and die.

How much more worthwhile to give the same dedication and sacrifice and attention to knowing God. Paul urges us to live life in God the way an athlete does: "So I run with purpose in every step. I am not just shadowboxing. I discipline my body like an athlete, training it to do what it should" (1 Corinthians 9:26-27).

In his essay *The Weight of Glory*, C. S. Lewis said that almost all of our modern philosophies are aimed at convincing us that our chief good is to be found in this life, on this earth. All this consumer society holds dear would convince us of the same thing. But the gospel of Christ insists that we were made for much more and far better than this present world can offer. The contemplation of death can force us into a clarity about the limitations of this life and open our eyes to see that in fact we were made for a glory that far exceeds the best things we now see. (That will be the theme of a later chapter.) So Lewis urges us to consider the possibility of glory in the next life and to ponder the fact that, therefore, in this life, "there are no ordinary people. You have never talked to a mere mortal. Nations, cultures, arts, civilizations—these are mortal, and their life is to ours as the life of a gnat. But it is immortals whom we joke with, work with, marry, snub, and exploit—immortal horrors or everlasting splendors."[10] The stakes are very high, are they not?

The Cathedral of Milan has three doorways, each spanned by a magnificent arch. Inscribed over the arch on one side is, "All that pleases us is but for a moment." Carved underneath is a beautiful wreath of roses. Inscribed over the arch on the opposite side is, "All that which troubles us is but for a moment." Carved beneath is a cross. The inscription over the arch in the central doorway is, "That only is important which is eternal." The two side arches are about mere moments in time; the central arch is about eternity. But all three touch on the themes of the gospel message: God alone is eternal; he alone is permanent; he is our only home. Everything else is momentary, ephemeral, passing away. But oh! What glories there are inside the sanctuary, in the holy place!

[handwritten annotations in margins:]

very short lived

God - the same yesterday today & forever

Time, fashions, language all changes but God never changes — what He says Heb 13:8

Is 46:11 God's purpose & will He does & means what He says

CHAPTER 6

THE URGENCY

TELL THEM THERE IS NO HURRY

This is all the more urgent, for you know how late it is; time is running out.
Wake up, for our salvation is nearer now than when we first believed. The
night is almost gone; the day of salvation will soon be here. So remove your
dark deeds like dirty clothes, and put on the shining armor of right living.
ROMANS 13:11-12

Procrastination is the thief of time.
EDWARD YOUNG, *NIGHT THOUGHTS*

"LIFE IS DIFFICULT."[1]

Those were the very first words of M. Scott Peck's 1978
bestseller, *The Road Less Traveled*. And many critics raved at
his sagacity. Apparently it was a brand-new idea to them.
But it is a very old idea. The wise have always known that
the choice in life is not whether it will be hard but what kind
of hardness: the good kind or the bad kind. Jesus said the
good kind is to walk the hard and narrow road of devotion
to him, because it is the road to life. He said the bad kind is
the broad and easy road that the world and the enemy of our
souls offer; it starts off easy but ends in eternal death.

Therefore the most important question anybody will ever
ask is, *What must I do to be saved?* The decision has eternal
consequences. The second most important question is, *How
much time do I have to decide?*

Years ago a television news station showed film footage of a group of skydivers falling through the air. They were laughing and waving at each other and turning somersaults as they anticipated pulling the rip cords on their parachutes and floating to the earth below. They even appeared to be floating as they fell. But it was an illusion they dared not believe—if they did, in a matter of seconds they would slam to the earth at about 120 miles per hour.

One by one the camera recorded each man as he pulled his rip cord. Each man seemed to shoot back up into the sky from the perspective of the cameraman, who kept falling. Then it came time for the cameraman to pull his rip cord. The camera began to pan wildly across the sky and the ground that was rushing to meet him, and then it went black.

What apparently had happened was that the cameraman, who was also the instructor for the other skydivers and a veteran of hundreds of other jumps, had forgotten to pack his parachute. In his preoccupation over getting the other men ready and his camera set to record their jump—both important things—he had forgotten the most important thing: to get himself ready, to take account of where he was headed at the end of the jump. What we saw in the film was the last thing he saw on earth.

CHRONOS AND KAIROS

One way to think about this disaster is as a fatal distraction. Skydiving had become routine to the cameraman; taking pictures of men skydiving was new and exciting. The new and exciting had diverted his attention away from the old and essential.

Another way to think about it is as a failure of timing. The Greeks had two words for time: *chronos* and *kairos*. One of these words is virtually absent from the Bible; the other is everywhere. *Chronos* means time as seen from a quantitative, linear perspective, time on a clock. *Kairos* means time as seen from the perspective of its quality and meaning, time as a season. To contrast the two, *chronos* time is concrete, *kairos* time is abstract; *chronos* is a date, *kairos* is a period, a *time*; *chronos* is something to manage and control, *kairos* is something to understand and obey; *chronos* passes, *kairos* is fulfilled. The Bible has practically no interest in time as *chronos* but is preoccupied with time as *kairos*. No wisdom is required to know what the *chronos* is—any fool can look at the numbers on a clock. But knowing what those numbers mean, their larger context, their *kairos*, is wisdom.

The man who forgot to pack his parachute probably knew exactly what the *chronos* was when he climbed into the airplane. It was the scheduled time to take off and jump; the numbers on the clock said so. But he had forgotten what the *kairos* was: It was time to take care of the most important thing a skydiver must do—pack the parachute before the *chronos* indicated it was time to jump. The *kairos* should have ruled the *chronos*; as it turned out, the opposite happened.

Jesus chided his contemporaries for knowing how to predict what the weather would be like tomorrow but being clueless about what time it was that day: "You know the saying, 'Red sky at night means fair weather tomorrow; red sky in the morning means foul weather all day.' You know how to interpret the weather signs in the sky, but you don't know how to interpret the signs of the times!" (Matthew 16:2-3). The word translated "times" is the plural of *kairos*. They were more concerned about the state of the weather than the state of their souls and the meaning of their times. They were taking pictures when they should have been packing their parachutes. This made Jesus mad, but mainly it made him grieve. On the Sunday before the Friday he was crucified, as he approached Jerusalem and looked at the city from a distance, he broke into sobs because he saw what was coming to the city in just a few decades. There would come a destruction so savage and cruel and so complete that later, as he carried his cross, he told grieving women not to weep for his suffering, but to weep for themselves and what they would suffer in that day. And why would the people suffer so? "Because you did not recognize the time [*kairos*] of God's coming to you" (Luke 19:44, NIV). Quite literally, children would die because they didn't know the time, the *kairos*.

KNOW YOUR TIME

Socrates said wisdom was knowing yourself. Jesus and the writers of Holy Scripture said wisdom is knowing your time, your *kairos*. *Kairos* was what Jesus had in mind when he responded to a bystander's question, "Master, will only a few be saved?" His answer was to tell the questioner to go after salvation with *agon*—the way a sprinter sprints to the finish line or a fighter fights a fight: "A bystander said, 'Master, will only a few be saved?' He said, 'Whether few or many is none of your business. Put your mind on your life with God. The way to life—to God!—is vigorous and requires your total attention'" (Luke 13:23-24, *The Message*).

Wisdom is knowing your time, your *kairos*.

One of the reasons Jesus said this is because the stakes are so high. One doesn't act nonchalantly when eternity is riding on decisions made in this life.

Nor does one waste time. *"For many,"* says Jesus, *"will try to enter but will fail"* (Luke 13:24, italics mine). On the surface, it sounds as if Jesus envisions a traffic jam at the door to heaven—it's a very narrow door; there are millions of people pushing and shoving to get in; but only the very strong and spiritually competitive will make it. But Jesus has something else in mind.

He explains what he means with a brief parable about a party. A whole village has been invited to a feast, maybe a wedding. The invitations were sent out, the time was announced, and when the party was to begin, the doors were closed the way doors to a concert hall are closed when a concert begins. In the parable, the latecomers are left outside knocking and begging to be let in. But they are treated as party crashers and strangers. The lord of the manor even calls them evildoers.

*When the master of the house has locked the door, it
will be too late. You will stand outside knocking and
pleading, "Lord, open the door for us!" But he will
reply, "I don't know you or where you come from." Then
you will say, "But we ate and drank with you, and you
taught in our streets." And he will reply, "I tell you, I
don't know you or where you come from. Get away from
me, all you who do evil."* (Luke 13:25-27)

THE NARROW DOOR IS TIME

The narrow door is time. It's not sinners who can't get in, for
all are invited. These are the very people Jesus came to seek
and save. The door is shut, not to the sinners but to the slackers, to the complacent and indolent who don't bother to actually read the invitation! Time runs out for these people, and
they are left standing outside, thrown out of the Kingdom
where "there will be weeping and gnashing of teeth" (Luke
13:28). Jesus doesn't say how good a runner or fighter one
has to be to get into the Kingdom—just that you must enter
the Kingdom with the abandon and urgency of a fighter or
a runner.

So of course the question of how much time we have
to respond to God's invitation is of paramount importance.
How much time do you have to decide about heaven or hell?
A lifetime, you say? How long is a lifetime? You don't know?
That is precisely the point. No one knows how much time
they have. But we do know this: time will run out. What

tragic foolishness, then, not to live wisely in the present in light of what is sure to come in the future.

The pastor of the church I grew up in would often try to impress us with the urgency of deciding now, not tomorrow, to follow Christ. His favorite way to apply pressure was to say, "You don't know whether, as you walk out of this sanctuary, you will be hit by a truck and sent hurtling into eternity. You might die tonight." I hated it when he did that. It was so manipulative. And it was so true, so very true. Often, as he finished his appeal, I would be checking my watch to see what the *chronos* was, thinking about lunch, and what time the game would be on TV that afternoon, and grousing inwardly that the service was going longer than usual, fifteen minutes longer. But I had no idea what time it was. The apostle Paul could have set me straight; he would have told me that the time, the *kairos*, was simply "now."

> *Don't squander one bit of this marvelous life God has given us. God reminds us,*
> *I heard your call in the nick of time;*
> *The day you needed me, I was there to help.*
> *Well, now is the right time to listen, the day to be helped. Don't put it off; don't frustrate God's work by showing up late.* (2 Corinthians 6:1-2, *The Message*)

One afternoon I sat with an elderly woman in my office. She was in her early seventies and was beautiful, physically. Had I not known her age, I would have guessed her to be in her late fifties. I recall the *chronos* was 1:00 p.m. We were discussing church membership. She had been attending our new-member seminar in order to explore whether she should join our church. She really liked the people, she told me, and she loved my sermons. (So far, I thought she would make a splendid church member!) Then she said, "But I don't believe Jesus is God incarnate. I believe in God, but Jesus just seems to me to be a good man, a prophet, perhaps. Besides, it's God I'm looking for—why should I have to go through Jesus? When I go shopping I want to talk to the manager, not the sales clerk." I had never heard that comparison before. But I had noticed that she was always dressed very stylishly.

We discussed the matter for quite a while, heatedly at times, but she wouldn't budge on the question of Jesus. This was more than just a speed bump on her way to church membership! The very idea of a church is based on the confession that Jesus Christ is the Son of God. So I finally told her that now wasn't the time for her to join the church but that I hoped she would keep coming.

Her face darkened. She was clearly upset that I wouldn't let her join. She got up rather abruptly and muttered something about not being sure if she would be coming back. It was a sad and sobering moment, to see someone reject Christ's offer of salvation so decisively. It got sadder and more sobering. Two hours later I received an urgent telephone call from her daughter, telling me her mother had just had a massive stroke and was in the hospital. Would I visit her? I did, and when the nurse let me into the room in ICU where this lady was hooked up to life support systems, I took one look and knew she was gone. She was pronounced dead an hour later.

As I stood there praying for her, I looked at my watch. The time was 4:30 p.m. Just a little over two hours had passed since I saw her walk out of my office confirmed, it seemed, in unbelief and destined to perish. I don't know what may have transpired between her and God between the time I last saw her and the time of her stroke, but the cry of my heart was, *Oh! That she changed her mind about the Lover and Savior of her soul!* What time did I say it was when we sat down to talk about the deity of Christ? 1:00 p.m.?

TELL THEM THERE IS NO HURRY

Remember, the question "Lord, will only a few be saved?" is a question about life or death, heaven or hell, forever. To grasp this fully is to realize that now is the time to decide and to wait not a second longer to go after salvation with *agon*, to go after God and his Kingdom with the fierce and vehement passion of one who knows that eternity hinges on what we do with the time we have now. The right time is now; the wrong time is later. The fight is begun; the race is on; the battle is raging. You're in it, whether you like it or not. The stakes are the highest and the door is narrow—the time short and uncertain.

It is said that Satan once called to him the emissaries of hell and said he wanted to send one of them to earth to aid women and men in the ruination of their souls. He asked which one wanted to go.

Now is the time to decide to go after salvation with *agon*, to go after God and his Kingdom with the fierce and vehement passion of one who knows that eternity hinges on what we do with the time we have now.

One creature came forward and said, "I will go." Satan said, "If I send you, what will you tell the children of men?" He said, "I will tell the children of men that there is no heaven." Satan said, "They will not believe you, for there is a bit of heaven in every human heart. In the end everyone knows that right and good must have the victory. You may not go."

Then another came forward, darker and fouler than the first. Satan said, "If I send you, what will you tell the children of men?" He said, "I will tell them there is no hell." Satan looked at him and said, "Oh, no; they will not believe you, for in every human heart there's a thing called conscience, an inner voice, which testifies to the truth that not only will good be triumphant, but evil will be defeated. You may not go."

Then one last creature came forward, this one from the darkest place of all. Satan said to him, "And if I send you, what will you say to women and men to aid them in the destruction of their souls?" He said, "I will tell them there is no hurry." Satan said, "Go!"[2]

CHAPTER 7

THE PRIZE

THE SPLENDORS OF GOD

So I run with purpose in every step. I am not just shadowboxing. I discipline my body like an athlete, training it to do what it should. Otherwise, I fear that after preaching to others I myself might be disqualified.
THE APOSTLE PAUL, IN 1 CORINTHIANS 9:26-27

He is no fool who gives what he cannot keep to gain that which he cannot lose.
JIM ELLIOT

ERNEST SHACKLETON, the audacious Antarctic explorer, ran an ad in a London newspaper in the early part of the twentieth century:

> Men wanted for hazardous journey. Small wages, bitter cold, long months of complete darkness, constant danger, safe return doubtful.

As unappealing as that may sound, the trip itself turned out to be even worse than advertised. Shackleton and his men set sail in August 1915, bound for an excursion over the Antarctic tundra. By October 1915, their ship, the *Endurance*, had become trapped in shifting ice and soon began to break up under the extreme pressure. Shackleton and his crew abandoned ship and temporarily set up camp on a series of ice floes, moving onto a new one whenever their floe crumbled against the deadly pack ice. Months later, when they finally spotted land on the horizon, they set out across the open sea in three small lifeboats. After seven harrowing days in savage weather and waters, they landed on Elephant Island, only to discover that it was just slightly more hospitable than the ice floes they had left behind.

Shackleton then decided to risk another longer and more dangerous open-boat journey to South Georgia Island. This time just one boat and six men would go; the rest of the crew would remain camped in the frozen waste of Elephant Island, waiting for help to come. They sealed the strongest of the lifeboats, which was named the *James Caird* in honor of the expedition's sponsor, with oil paint and seal's blood and set out for South Georgia Island. Shackleton knew that if the journey took more than a month, the boat and its crew would be lost, so he packed enough supplies for only four weeks. But they made the crossing in seventeen days, wrestling with seas that threatened constantly to capsize the little lifeboat and enduring a hurricane that sank a five-hundred-ton steamer.

After some difficulty procuring a rescue ship, Shackleton returned to Elephant Island to retrieve the rest of his crew. It had been four months since the *James Caird* had left, and the men had all but given up hope of rescue when they saw their captain returning for them. Perhaps most amazing of all, throughout the entire ordeal, not a single man in Shackleton's crew lost his life.

THE SPLENDORS OF GOD AND THE NAKED SOUL OF MEN

Perhaps it was on this journey that Shackleton gave the world this hair-raising anecdote: "I called to the other men that the sky was clearing, and then a moment later I realized that what I had seen was not a rift in the clouds but the white crest of an enormous wave."

So what was the response to the ad in the London newspaper? It was overwhelming; inquiries poured in. Shackleton said, "It seemed as though all the men in Great Britain were determined to accompany me."

Although these men had no idea their trip would turn out to be so perilous—or so lengthy—they weren't naïve about the risks involved; they knew they were volunteering for a dangerous voyage. Why would anybody want to travel with somebody like Shackleton? Were there just a lot of jaded and deluded men in England who could think of nothing better to do than to make low wages and live in bitter cold and constant danger? Perhaps. But more likely, they wanted to experience something of what Shackleton said happened to the souls of those who went on these expeditions. Looking back on all they had done, he said, "We had seen God in his splendors, heard the text that Nature renders. We had reached the naked soul of men."[1]

That's what they signed up for; that's what they wanted. To travel with Shackleton would be the hardest challenge they had ever faced. But hardship and danger were small prices to pay if it meant seeing something of the splendors of God, hearing the voice of nature, and reaching the naked soul of men. They were glory seekers. They thought the high price was a bargain.

Paul said the Christian life was to be lived with the same outlook. After suffering a beating so severe that he was left for dead, Paul told the churches of Iconium, Lystra, and Pisidian Antioch, "We must suffer many hardships to enter the kingdom of God" (Acts 14:22). Read only from the hardship angle, that statement is a turnoff; why go on a journey that is hard, hazardous, and dark? Read from the perspective of the glories at the journey's end, it's an altogether different matter;

The high price of following Christ is really a bargain.

the path, though hard and narrow, leads to delights and glories in God's Kingdom that far outweigh whatever it costs to get there. The high price is really a bargain.

The martyr/missionary Jim Elliot understood this perfectly when, as a college student, he wrote in his diary, "He is no fool who gives what he cannot keep to gain that which he cannot lose." The price may be high, but it's a bargain. Jesus compared it to a treasure of such surpassing worth that those with eyes to see it would gladly give up all they own to get it, in the same way a farmer sells everything he owns for a field with buried treasure:

The kingdom of heaven is like treasure hidden in a field. When a man found it, he hid it again, and then in his joy went and sold all he had and bought that field.

Again, the kingdom of heaven is like a merchant looking for fine pearls. When he found one of great value, he went away and sold everything *he had and bought it.* (Matthew 13:44-46, NIV, emphasis mine)

TOO GRAND TO GRASP

What Paul said to the churches he got from Jesus, who said we must enter his Kingdom with *agon*, the same fierce abandon and vigor an athlete takes to a competition. How could it be otherwise? The Kingdom is the most important thing there is. "Christianity is a statement which, if false, is of no importance," wrote C. S. Lewis, "and, if true, is of infinite importance. The one thing it cannot be is moderately important."[2] That is why Lewis observed in another place that Jesus got only three reactions from people: hatred, terror, or adoration. The one response he never got was mild approval.[3] Jesus and his gospel are infinitely important, not to be believed mildly.

There are different kinds of hard when it comes to the Kingdom. There is the hardship, the *agon* of persecution, the kind of thing Paul told the believers in Iconium, Lystra, and Pisidian Antioch to be ready for. But there is another kind of *agon*—the *agon* of discipline, self-imposed hardship for the sake of the prize. Paul urged the Corinthian believers to live their lives like an athlete in strict training:

Don't you realize that in a race everyone runs, but only one person gets the prize? So run to win! All athletes are disciplined in their training. They do it to win a prize that will fade away, but we do it for an eternal prize. So I run with purpose in every step. I am not just shadowboxing. I discipline my body like an athlete, training it to do what it should. Otherwise, I fear that after preaching to others I myself might be disqualified. (1 Corinthians 9:24-27)

The point of strict training is not the training itself but the prize; discipline is a means, not an end. It's the prize that makes the discipline worth it. What is this prize? The language of the New Testament is so rich in metaphor and word pictures that it strains the intellect and imagination. For some, the reward of following Christ may seem too good to be true; for me it has always seemed too grand to grasp. The truest thing I can say about it is that "no eye has seen, no ear has heard, and no mind has imagined what God has prepared for those who love him" (1 Corinthians 2:9; cf. Isaiah 64:4, 65:17). I take that to mean that if I can think or imagine what it may be, it will automatically be better than I imagined. With that caveat, let me make a stab at understanding the prize. Near the end of his life, as he sat in a prison cell on death row, Paul looked back on his life and was satisfied that he had indeed lived the *agon*: he had fought the good fight and finished the race. What now? What did he have to look forward to after his

> It's the prize that makes the *agon* of discipline and self-imposed hardship worth it.

execution? "And now the prize awaits me—the crown of righteousness, which the Lord, the righteous Judge, will give me on the day of his return. And the prize is not just for me but for all who eagerly look forward to his appearing" (2 Timothy 4:8).

LET'S CELEBRATE TOGETHER

Whatever else the crown of righteousness may be, the one thing that stands out about it is the One who bestows it: the Lord, the righteous Judge. In other words, the great prize for which we have lived and longed our whole lives will in some way include being applauded and congratulated by God himself. Greater than the crown is the One who bestows the crown. That thought strikes a chord deep in my soul. The sweetest words I will ever hear will be God's: "Well done, my good and faithful servant. . . . Let's celebrate together!" (Matthew 25:21). We were made to want this—to be at home with God forever. Augustine was longing for this when he prayed, "You made us for yourself and our hearts find no peace until they rest in you."[4] Bernard of Clairvaux said it another way: "From the best bliss that life imparts, we turn unfilled to Thee again." There is a God-shaped vacuum in each of us that, when filled full, fulfills us.[5] Every human desire points ultimately to the heart's deepest desire: to see the smile of God.

I have a mental picture of what the divine accolade[6] and embrace may be like. One day when my children were small, I was dusting the furniture in my living room. Music was playing—Beethoven's *Fifth Symphony*, as I recall—and I began to move to the music as I worked. The more I worked and listened, the more vigorously and flamboyantly I danced. Thinking no one could see, I leapt and twirled through the room without embarrassment. Perhaps I should have been embarrassed, since I've been told I look a little like a bear on roller skates when I dance. But I was having fun.

Gradually I became aware of what actually felt like eyes looking at me—very little eyes. I looked and detected my four-year-old hiding behind the sofa watching his daddy dance so silly. He was beaming with delight. I looked around to see if anyone else was watching. No one was, so I invited him to join me in the dance. Around the room we danced a rough-and-tumble ballet—we leapt over chairs, ran across the coffee table, jumped up and down on the sofa—something he would normally be spanked for doing! We shouted and giggled and sang made-up arias in unknown languages. I finally had to sit down, exhausted. But he continued. I began to applaud his dance. I wish you could have seen the look of unabashed pleasure and joy on his face as he danced to his daddy's applause. He was acting as a true child of his father, receiving and giving pleasure as he danced with me and for me. He honored me with his joyful imitation, and I honored him with my applause.

Will it be a little like that when the righteous Judge crowns us? I don't know, but I think so. Maybe. Thoughts like that seem to explain a little the reason for the ache in my heart when I think of the prize—the thrill of fully pleasing the One I was made to please.

O Israel, rejoice in your Maker.
    O people of Jerusalem, exult in your King.
Praise his name with dancing,
    accompanied by tambourine and harp.
For the LORD *delights in his people.* (Psalm 149:2-4)

DAZZLING POSSIBILITIES

Jesus used another picture that resonates in my heart. He said that one day "the righteous will shine like the sun in their Father's Kingdom" (Matthew 13:43).

What can that mean? Will the brightness of our humanity be to what we are now as the sun is to other light—so much greater than what we are now that we can only squint to look at it? Is what we are now, the reflection of God in our humanness, a mere match compared to the sun of what we will be? Think of the way the sun dominates the sky and provides the gravitational center of the solar system; of how all the planets reflect its light and all living things draw life from it. Does Jesus mean that our glorification will be to the created order what the sun is to the solar system?

Will our freedom mean its freedom too? Are Paul's words in Romans 8 another way of depicting the same thing?

The whole creation is on tiptoe to see the wonderful sight of the sons of God coming into their own. . . . And the hope is that in the end the whole of created life will be rescued from the tyranny of change and decay, and have its share in that magnificent liberty which can only belong to the children of God! (Romans 8:18-19, 21, *Phillips*)

Will we discover that when we are set right, everything else will be set right too? Will babies put their hands in cobra dens and not be harmed? Will wolves and lambs lie down together and the lambs get a good night's sleep? Will we discover that the Dr. Doolittle stories were myth instead of fantasy, that one day our freedom will mean animals can talk human, or humans can talk animal? Will the trees really clap their hands for joy, and will we hear the music of the spheres? Will the highest mountains and the ocean depths and the deepest forests become home to us? Will the farthest reaches of the universe be ours to touch and explore—all because we have finally realized the full implications of what it means to be human beings? The possibilities are dazzling, like the sun.

I don't know if anything I've said here is anywhere near on target. Whatever the truth of my musings, we can be sure of this: When we see Jesus we will be like Jesus, who is "the radiance of God's glory" (Hebrews 1:3, NIV; see also 1 John 3:2). This hope purifies us, the Bible says.[7] And even though we don't see it yet, it fills us with "a glorious, inexpressible joy" because we know that we are receiving the goal of our faith, the salvation of our souls (1 Peter 1:8-9).

Shackleton claimed to have seen the splendor of God, heard the text of nature, and touched the naked soul of humanity on his adventures. We may forgive this gush of hyperbole as the words of a man understandably dazzled by the extremes of Antarctica, or overly impressed by his press clippings. Paul would certainly take sharp issue with him. And we know what Bernard of Clairvaux and Augustine would say. There are glories, and there is Glory: "For God, who said, 'Let there be light in the darkness,' has made this light shine in our hearts so we could know the glory of God that is seen in the face of Jesus Christ" (2 Corinthians 4:6). The splendor of God, indeed!

GOD'S GREAT COMPLAINT

God's great complaint about us is that we can so quickly and thoughtlessly give our hearts to the paltry and temporary glories of Shackleton adventures—or even less!—when there is so much more. When it comes to the enduring and expansive joys of the eternal crown, "we are half-hearted creatures." C. S. Lewis wrote:

> If we consider the unblushing promises of reward and the staggering nature of the rewards promised in the Gospels, it would seem that Our Lord finds our desires not too strong, but too weak. We are half-hearted creatures, fooling about with drink and sex and ambition when infinite joy is offered us, like an ignorant child who wants to go on making mud pies in a slum because he cannot imagine what is meant

by the offer of a holiday at the sea. We are far too easily pleased.[8]

John Newton, the author of "Amazing Grace," chided Christians who lose this perspective on the way to heaven because the way is grueling. He said they are like a man traveling to New York to take possession of a great estate but whose carriage breaks down en route so that he has to walk the rest of the way. "What a fool we should think him, if we saw him wringing his hands, and blubbering out all the remaining mile, 'My [carriage] is broken! My [carriage] is broken!'"[9]

God's great complaint about us is that we can so quickly and thoughtlessly give our hearts to paltry and temporary glories.

That being the case, we can do the hard things of this life with a profound sense of joy and peace because we know "our present troubles are small and won't last very long. Yet they produce for us a glory that vastly outweighs them and will last forever!" (2 Corinthians 4:17).

PART 3

THE OBSTACLES

YOU HAVE ENEMIES: THE FLESH,
THE WORLD, AND THE DEVIL

MY FIRST SPIRITUAL CRISIS came the last evening of a summer church camp I attended when I was thirteen years old. As the crisis came to a head, I was sitting nervously in the shadows of the back row of a campfire circle.

All that week the speaker had been urging those of us who had been trusting Christ as Savior to now begin obeying him as Lord. The distinction he made between Christ as Savior and Christ as Lord was, at best, an overzealous application of the doctrine of salvation through faith alone, not by works. At worst, it was heresy. But it was what he believed in and what I had lived by.

That night at the campfire, I was wrestling with something I had always known in my heart to be true: You can't take Jesus in bits and pieces, Savior now and Lord later. I was beginning to see that being with Jesus was much more than a free pass to heaven. All I could think of that night was that if I yielded to his lordship, it would probably mean two things: he would veto my desire to be a cartoonist, and he would make me marry Stephanie Osgood (an alias). Stephanie was a girl in my church who my mother told me "would make somebody a sweet wife." I got the message—though I had absolutely no attraction to her. If I were serious about God, though, I'd have to get serious about her and marry her. It never occurred to me that she might not want to marry me either. But that was what I believed was at stake that night, if I were to walk down to the campfire and declare before about a hundred people my intention to obey Christ as Lord.

Before this cloud of witnesses, the camp speaker would ask me, "Will you do whatever Jesus asks you to do?"

I would answer, "Yes."

He then would ask, "Will you go wherever he sends you?"

I would say, "Yes." And then I would throw a piece of wood into the fire, as a symbol of my life, an offering to God.

When it came time to close the deal that night, that's what I did, tremblingly. In case you're interested, I soon lost all desire to be a cartoonist; and as I write this, I am in my fortieth year of marriage to a woman I am definitely attracted to—definitely. And her name is Lauretta, not Stephanie.

But all that is beside the point. My struggle that night was not about vocation and marriage; those were just the arenas where the real struggle took place. The real struggle was between Jesus and me: which of us would be boss? Following Christ was not about whether to be a cartoonist or to marry a particular person. It was about whether I would be willing to become the new person—the new creation, actually—that following Christ would make me.

There are enemies and obstacles to this change, known classically as the devil, the world, and what the Bible calls my "flesh," or the old me. All three were conspiring against me walking down to the campfire that night to offer myself to God totally. They are still at it. The devil is slick and seductive; the world, persuasive and overwhelming; but the toughest of them, the orneriest, silliest, and most stubborn of them all, is the old me.

CHAPTER 8

THE FOOL

MAKING JESUS THE HOMEBOY

Then you will say, "But we ate and drank with you, and you taught in our streets." And he will reply, "I tell you, I don't know you or where you come from. Get away from me, all you who do evil."
JESUS, IN LUKE 13:26-27

I asked for a God who should be as like me as possible. What use to me is a God whose divinity consists in doing difficult things that I cannot do or saying clever things that I cannot understand? The God I want and intend to get must be someone I can recognize immediately without having to wait and see what he says or does. There must be nothing in the least extraordinary about him. Produce him at once, please. I'm sick of waiting.
HEROD, IN W. H. AUDEN'S *FOR THE TIME BEING*

JESUS OPENS DOORS. He even declared that he is the Door and that what he opens no one can shut and what he shuts no one can open.[1] But he is not like the automatic door in a supermarket. A preschool Sunday school teacher was explaining to her class that even though they could not see him, Jesus was always with them. "I already know that," chirped a four-year-old. "He's the one who opens the door when we go into a store."[2]

Nothing is automatic with Jesus Christ. He makes hard and exacting discriminations about whom he lets into his Kingdom. Some will be refused entrance, and for the most surprising reason—not because they didn't believe there was a Kingdom, or didn't think it was a good thing or a desirable commodity, but because they didn't take it seriously. The Kingdom was never formally rejected, just demoted, marginalized. Instead of being infinitely important, a matter of life or death requiring their utmost attention, it was relegated to matters moderately important—one of the many good things they thought they might get around to someday.

A DREADFUL SURPRISE

But when "someday" comes, they are shocked to discover that the Master of the Kingdom has shut and locked the door, and they are standing outside, begging to be let in. Suddenly their priorities are set straight. What they once mildly approved of is what they now want more than life itself. But it is too late. Jesus warns them, "You will stand outside knocking and pleading, 'Lord, open the door for us!' But he will reply, 'I don't know you or where you come from'" (Luke 13:25).

Too late, they discover that there will be dreadful surprises in the Kingdom of God. What they thought belonged to them, doesn't; and those they were sure didn't belong, do. A friend of mine used to say that the two most often asked questions in the Kingdom will be, "What are you doing here?" and "Where is so-and-so?" That's not exactly the way Jesus put it, but it comes close:

There will be weeping and gnashing of teeth, for you will see Abraham, Isaac, Jacob, and all the prophets

in the Kingdom of God, but you will be thrown out.
And people will come from all over the world—from
east and west, north and south—to take their places in
the Kingdom of God. And note this: Some who seem
least important now will be the greatest then, and some
who are the greatest now will be least important then.
(Luke 13:28-30)

So Jesus said to go after his Kingdom with *agonizomai*, with the focus and intensity of an athlete running a race, the vehement determination of a wrestler fighting an opponent. There can be no half-measures, no complacency. The stakes are the highest, and the time is uncertain. Something as important as life or death for eternity demands our utmost for his highest.[3]

JESUS THE HOMEBOY

What kind of person would be so foolish, so recklessly negligent, to miss something as important as this? With one deft stroke, Jesus reveals their character. It's in what they say to the master of the house when he won't let them in: "But we ate and drank with you, and you taught in our streets" (Luke 13:26).

We *know you.* You *know us.* They thought Jesus was a homeboy, a neighbor, part of the community, a member of the club—of which, of course, they also were already members. He was their guy. Their assumption was: *Salvation? It's a done deal. I'm in. I'm here. He's here. It's cool. How many of us will there be?* But they don't know him at all. Worse, he doesn't know them. Eugene Peterson translates these lines, "You'll protest, 'But we've known you all our lives!' only to be interrupted with his abrupt, 'Your kind of knowing can hardly be called knowing. You don't know the first thing about me'" (Luke 13:26-27, *The Message*).

There is a term for this kind of bogus faith: *nominal Christianity*, meaning "in name only." Rather than seeing the jaw-dropping, amazing grace and miracle that it is, they saw salvation as a birthright, their place in the Kingdom as a given, a right to be claimed—which meant, of course, that salvation was no longer salvation but entitlement. They didn't need to be saved, just given what belonged to them. Salvation was a piece of property, a label, a family name—not a life or death decision.

For nominal Christians, faith in Jesus is like the old ad for Coca-Cola: *Things Go Better with Coke.* The slogan was usually accompanied by a picture of a juicy hamburger and french fries on a plate, with a frosty Coca-Cola sitting nearby, the perfect complement to a great meal, bringing out the best in your burger. For nominal Christians, Jesus is a side dish, not the entree; an enhancement, not the essential; an accessory, not standard equipment; a spoke, not the hub; a supplement; a complement. Life is better with him than without him, to be sure, but it won't end if he goes away. They'd be sad, but not devastated.

> For nominal Christians, Jesus is an enhancement, not the essential.

WHAT MAKES JESUS WANT TO THROW UP

Nominal Christians are lukewarm Christians, which should give us pause. Lost sinners made Jesus weep; hypocrites made him fume; but lukewarm Christians made him want to throw up. That's a bit of an exaggeration. What he actually says to them is what he said to the church at Laodicea, in the book of Revelation: "I know all the things you do, that you are neither hot nor cold. I wish that you were one or the other! But since you are like lukewarm water, neither hot nor cold, I will spit you out of my mouth!" (Revelation 3:15-16).

I will spit you out of my mouth! Just about anyone can understand the Lord's aversion to lukewarm water, because nearly everyone has tasted it. Tepid water is the worst kind; better hot or cold than lukewarm. It's disgusting. Spit it out!

Many have misinterpreted this saying to mean that Jesus would rather we be either hot in our faith (as in zealous) or even cold (as in indifferent) than blandly religious. Anything is better than an insipid, domesticated faith, right? That's not what he is saying. What he is saying is that the faith of the church at Laodicea is like their city's water supply. Neighboring Colossae was noted for its cold, refreshing river water. Nearby Hierapolis was famous for its healing hot springs. People traveled great distances to soak in them. But unlike Colossae and Hierapolis, Laodicea had no indigenous

Lost sinners made Jesus weep; hypocrites made him fume; but lukewarm Christians made him want to throw up.

water supply. Its water came by aqueduct from six miles away. The long journey under the sun made it brackish and luke-warm. It tasted awful. So Jesus was saying to the Laodicean believers that he wished they were either cold and refreshing like the water of Colossae or hot and healing like the water of Hierapolis. As it was, they were neither refreshing nor healing, just blah, listless, and lifeless. Their water came to them secondhand.

Laodicea has become synonymous with nominal Christianity. Like its water, its faith is so far removed from the Source that it barely qualifies as faith at all. One of the first steps down the slippery slope of nominal Christianity is to begin to talk more *about* Jesus than *to* him—which is to say that your prayer life begins to shrink. Sermons and studies are essential, but if they are all you do, or even most of what you do, their effect is to reduce Jesus to a distant presence, an impersonal object—to demote him from the vital and unsettling Presence that he is to a mere idea and ideal.

One of the first steps down the slippery slope of nominal Christianity is to begin to talk more *about* Jesus than *to* him.

The goal of preaching and teaching is to lead you to more and deeper conversations with Christ. When God speaks through his Word, you must answer—in praise, confession, and obedience. If you don't, he gets pushed outside your life and outside the church. Imagine a husband who speaks personally and passionately to his wife about matters of great importance to their marriage and in return gets only a nod of agreement but no engagement, assent but no response. That's a picture of a church with nominal faith. This is a church that Jesus asks to be let back into! He's not inside the church but outside, knocking on the door: "Look! I stand at the door and knock. If you hear my voice and open the door, I will come in, and we will share a meal together as friends" (Revelation 3:20).

Jesus wants to connect with the nominal Christian in a deep, personal way—the way close friends do when they sit around a table to enjoy a long, leisurely meal together. Or the way a vine connects to its branches. He is the Vine, and we are the branches; apart from him we can do nothing but shrivel up and die (see John 15:1-6).

The metaphors are starting to multiply. Jesus is to us like fresh, living water; like a dear friend sharing a great meal; or like a vine feeding its branches. There are many more in Scripture, but they are all pictures of the same thing: vital, intimate contact with God. William Wilberforce used yet another metaphor; he said the nominal Christian sees "the truths of the Gospel . . . like distant stars that twinkle with a vain and idle luster." They are true but far away; verities to ponder but not the light that gives life, the sun of existence. "But to the real Christian," these truths are "the center in which he gravitates, like the sun of his system, and the source of his light, warmth, and life."[4]

FEELING GOD'S PLEASURE

Jesus urges us to enter the Kingdom of God the way a runner runs a race or a wrestler wrestles an opponent; with exuberance and determination, fierce earnestness and passion. *Agonizomai.* The nominal Christian cannot understand this, much less do it. In order to run the race and fight the good fight with "light, warmth, and life" in our souls, we must not only run the *way* Jesus ran the race, using him as a model, but *with* Jesus, as a companion, in the power of his Spirit!

> *Therefore, since we are surrounded by such a huge crowd of witnesses to the life of faith, let us strip off every weight that slows us down, especially the sin that so easily trips us up. And let us run with endurance the race God has set before us. We do this by keeping our eyes on Jesus, the champion who initiates and perfects our faith. Because of the joy awaiting him, he endured the cross, disregarding its shame. Now he is seated in the place of honor beside God's throne.* (Hebrews 12:1-2)

Keeping our eyes on Jesus. What does that mean? It doesn't mean watching the race as a spectator but running the race as a contender. The temptation of nominal Christianity is to see the gift of Christ's Kingdom the way a ticket holder sees a ticket to the Olympic Games. Getting into heaven is like getting past the box office, through the turnstile, and into the stands. No! To get into heaven is to be assigned a number and given a pass into the stadium to compete. It's to be given the permission and the power to run and fight, like Paul did, to "work and struggle . . . depending on Christ's mighty power that works within me" (Colossians 1:29). Be assured of this: Jesus is not in the stands;

he's on the field. Look for him there in the sweat and heat of the struggle—that's how to keep your eyes on Jesus.

No wonder nominal Christianity is such an enemy of *agonizomai*. It is Christianity without Christ and therefore without the acute joy and painful pleasure of running with him.

The film *Chariots of Fire* won the Academy Award for best picture in 1981. It was based on the story of two British runners who competed in the 1924 Olympics. One of them, Eric Liddell, was a devout Christian. As he prepared for the Olympic games, he was known as one of the best sprinters in the world—as well as for his capacity for *agonizomai*.

Once Liddell was knocked down early in a 440-yard race. He sat for a moment on the track dazed, until he heard someone yell, "Get up!" He jumped up, and though he was twenty yards behind the others, he fought his way through the rest of the pack and won the race.

Eric's heart was set on going to the mission field in China after the Olympics. But his sister Jennie saw this delay as putting running ahead of serving God and called his commitment into question. The movie provides a snapshot of the conversation in which Eric tried to explain to her why he runs. Smiling, he announced,

"I've decided I'm going back to China. . . ."

Jennie interrupted him. "Oh, Eric, I'm so pleased."

He continued, "But I've got a lot of running to do first. Jennie, you've got to understand. I believe that God made me for a purpose, for China. He also made me fast, and when I run, *I feel his pleasure.* To give it up would be to hold him in contempt. You were right; it's not just fun. To win is to honor him."[5]

God's pleasure, his praise, his approval—the greatest words we will ever hear, and the greatest pleasure we will ever know, will be at the end of our days when the Master says of our lives, of the fight we have fought and the race we have run, "Well done, good and faithful servant. . . . Enter into the joy of your master" (Matthew 25:21, ESV).

The second greatest pleasure is hearing him whisper it in our ears right now. This explains the crazy attitude so many Christians have toward suffering and hardship. If it means being with Jesus—hearing his voice and seeing his smile—it is worth it, whatever the distress and deprivation, no matter how hard. The great Aaronic blessing, spoken countless times over the people of God, is about that very thing, the knowledge and experience of God's pleasure, his smile:

> *May the LORD bless you*
>   *and protect you.*
> *May the LORD smile on you*
>   *and be gracious to you.*
> *May the LORD show you his favor*
>   *and give you his peace.* (Numbers 6:24-26)

We were created to crave that smile, that closeness with our Creator.

CHAPTER 9

THE COST

EASY TO PLEASE, HARD TO SATISFY

But now you must be holy in everything you do, just as God who chose you is holy. For the Scriptures say, "You must be holy because I am holy."
1 PETER 1:15-16

O Love, ever burning, never extinguished, O Charity, my God, set me on fire!
. . . Give what you command, and then command whatever you will.
AUGUSTINE, *THE CONFESSIONS*

I'VE HAD A succession of favorite Jesus pictures over the years. In my youth, in the 1940s and 50s, it was the Warner Sallman head of Jesus on the frontispiece of my Bible: a handsome man, a gentle Nordic type, certainly not a Palestinian Jew. With his long, shimmering brown hair, square jaw, aristocratic nose, and broad forehead, I rather hoped I would grow up to look like him. The last I checked, more than 500 million copies of this painting have been reproduced, and I still don't look like him. Jesus, the movie star.[1]

Then came the radical 60s and student rebellion. Antiestablishment sentiments ran strong then. My favorite picture of Jesus showed him sitting in church, slumped over, *asleep*. His mouth was open, and he was probably snoring. He was bored with church, just like I was; contemptuous of its foibles and hypocrisy, just like I was. His hair was longer than the Sallman Jesus, jet black and scraggly. It didn't shimmer but gleamed with the oil that had accumulated from infrequent washings. Just like mine. Jesus, the hippie.

In the 70s, another picture captured my fancy. It showed Jesus cracking up. That's right, his head was thrown back, and he was laughing. It was just a head shot, but I was sure he had a cool drink in his hand. Just like I did. He was a fun guy. I wanted to hang out with him. He reminded me of my buddies. Jesus, the dude.

I don't keep pictures of Jesus anymore. It dawned on me after my Jesus the Dude phase that it wasn't Jesus I was interested in as much as it was what I believed, and what I hoped he stood for. I could have learned that lesson from my theological studies. Historically, most of the people who have so passionately wanted to get at the "real" Jesus, the historical Jesus, to uncover the figure behind the accretions of tradition and "churchianity," ended up finding the same thing. What they found was a Jesus who looked a lot like them. The biblical word for what they (and I) were looking for is *idol*. Idols are God-substitutes, false gods.

A LOVE THAT CONFRONTS

Idolatry is what lies at the heart of nominal Christianity. There is a saying: "God made us in his own image, and we've been returning the favor ever since"—trying to make him in our image. But idolatry is not just the particular sin of nominal Christianity; it's the essence of all sin. We sinners don't want a God who confronts us with who he is; we want a god who confirms us in who we are.

Tom Landry, the legendary coach of the Dallas Cowboys, defined a coach as one who makes men do what they don't want to do so they may become what they want to be. How

> We sinners don't want a God who confronts us with who he is; we want a god who confirms us in who we are.

much more is that the way it is with God! As sinners we seek an *agon*-less god who requires no change, no struggle. With this god there is no need for change because this god has no existence outside our minds. He's a solipsism.

The real God, the true and living God, is something else. He is a confronter. The real God is all about *agon*, because the real God wants to make us real too, and that requires change. It is the nature of his love, because his love is a holy love; he loves us just as we are, but he loves us too much to let us stay that way. His love is, "Love to the loveless shown/ That they might lovely be."[2] His love is "a consuming fire" (Hebrews 12:29, NIV); and his command is "You must be holy because I am holy" (1 Peter 1:16). "To ask that God's love should be content with us as we are," wrote C. S. Lewis, "is to ask that God should cease to be God":

> Because He is what He is, His love must, in the nature of things, be impeded and repelled by certain stains in our present character, and because He already loves us He must labor to make us lovable. We cannot even

wish, in our better moments, that He should reconcile Himself to our present impurities.[3]

[So God's holy love] may forgive all infirmities and love still in spite of them: but Love cannot cease to will their removal. Love is more sensitive than hatred itself to every blemish in the beloved. . . . Of all powers he forgives most, but he condones least: he is pleased with little, but demands all.[4]

When he became a Christian, George MacDonald thought of his life as a house that needed repairs. The roof was leaking, the porch was sagging, and the windows were cracked; he had a bad temper, a lust problem, and a few other vices growing like weeds in the garden. He expected Jesus to make the necessary repairs. What he got was *agon*: Jesus didn't repair anything—he tore the house down, dug up the foundation, and began all over again! Jesus' goal is never to remodel but to rebuild. He wants us to be glorious, not so-so.

NOT FOR THE HEALTHY

God's demand for holiness and glory can sound harsh and perfectionistic, like the callous "fitness" tests that were once given to immigrants at Ellis Island. Though thousands of immigrants entered the United States through Ellis Island in the nineteenth and early twentieth centuries, some were turned back soon after they arrived, because the United States government did not want the feebleminded, tubercular, or those with other lung diseases and glaucoma to enter the country. One of the ways doctors would determine who had bad eyes or lungs or was mentally handicapped was to have all immigrants walk up several flights of stairs to an examination area. I'm physically fit, but when I visited Ellis Island and climbed those stairs I was out of breath when I got to the top. In those days doctors would stand at the top of the stairs to see who was stumbling and wheezing or otherwise laboring to make their way up the stairs. These individuals would be pulled out of the crowd, away from their families, and sent back to the boats. It must have been heartwrenching to see. Spiritually, it can seem that God is like a doctor scrutinizing us from the top of the stairs, and we are all blind and tubercular, struggling and stumbling our way to failure. Who can possibly be holy as he is holy?

But imagine one of those doctors spying a man coughing and wheezing his way up the stairs, blind and groping for help. The doctor runs down the stairs to the man, picks him up, and helps him the rest of the way to the examination area. Then he administers food and antibiotics and checks him into a hospital, personally covering all his expenses. When he is released, he takes him into his home and includes him as a member of his family. That would be like God. The demand was still there: health remained a requirement. But with the requirement came also the means to meet the requirement.

God's demand for holiness is total. He does command perfection. Jesus said, "You are to be perfect, even as your Father in heaven is perfect" (Matthew 5:48). Yet it's a perfection that is radically different from the kind practiced on Ellis Island. There one had to be healthy to be let in. But the unhealthy are precisely the people Jesus is looking for. He explained his mission by saying, "Healthy people don't need a doctor— sick people do" (Matthew 9:12). His passion, quite literally, is to make the unhealthy, healthy—that is, holy. We may want house repairs, but God wants an extreme makeover. He's not interested in making us better people; he wants to make us a new creation.

"God," George MacDonald said, "is easy to please, but hard to satisfy."[6] Like the loving father he is, he is pleased with our feeblest efforts to grow. We know how this works— parents have been known to break into wild applause when their baby takes a first step. But they won't be satisfied until their child can walk as a mature adult. They want it all. Though easily pleased, all good parents are hard to satisfy. God is our Creator; his vision of perfection is simply that we become all he created us to be, and he won't be satisfied until we are. And what is that? We are to be like his Son, Jesus, the Son who gives us the right to be called his brothers and sisters— sons and daughters of God:[7]

> **God's passion is to make the unhealthy, healthy—that is, holy. He's not interested in making us better people; he wants to make us a new creation.**

> *Dear friends, we are already God's children, but he has not yet shown us what we will be like when Christ*

appears. But we do know that we will be like him, for we will see him as he really is. (1 John 3:2)

And the Lord—who is the Spirit—makes us more and more like him as we are changed into his glorious image. (2 Corinthians 3:18)

GIVE WHAT YOU COMMAND

Augustine understood this when he prayed, "Give what you command, and then command whatever you will." This is the promise prophesied in Ezekiel:

And I will give you a new heart, and I will put a new spirit in you. I will take out your stony, stubborn heart and give you a tender, responsive heart. And I will put my Spirit in you so that you will follow my decrees and be careful to obey my regulations. (Ezekiel 36:26-27)

It is the grace celebrated by the psalmist who prayed, "I run in the path of your commands, for you have broadened my understanding" (Psalm 119:32, NIV). The process of learning to run is long and hard, and sometimes painful. But it's a good hard, not a bad hard.

The power of God's grace is a mystery. One way to begin to understand it is to see it as simply his acceptance of us, just as we are, unconditionally, through our faith in Christ:

But God showed his great love for us by sending Christ
to die for us while we were still sinners. (Romans 5:8)

God saved you by his grace when you believed. And
you can't take credit for this; it is a gift from God.
(Ephesians 2:8)

That truth alone is transforming, life-changing. If this
were all God's grace was, it would be wonderful enough. God
knows how we humans come alive in trust. He should—he
made us that way. He also knows how we wilt when there is
no trust.

Think of it for a moment, on a purely human level. Do
you know people who, when you are around them, bring out
your worst? I know someone who I feel always looks at me
through squinty, critical eyes. My belief regarding his belief
about me is that he sees me as oafish, shallow, and arrogant.
I can't prove he sees me that way, but my experience of him
has led me to believe, right or wrong, that he does. So how
do I act when I am around him? To my great frustration and
embarrassment, I often find myself saying and doing things
that are, in fact, oafish, shallow, and arrogant. The harder I
try not to be what I think he believes I am, the more I end
up being that way!

When I am around him, it's like my experience as a baseball player in middle school. I had a bad reputation as a
baseball player; I just couldn't get the hand-eye coordination
thing right. In later years, my success as an athlete would be

mainly playing games in which I could knock people down. But baseball required finesse. Fly balls would come my way, and I would sometimes miss them by a foot; or if they hit my hands, they would bounce out. I was always the last player chosen when teams were forming at recess or after school. Guys hated to have me on their team. It got so bad that when a ball was hit my way, my teammates would immediately start screaming for me not to drop it. My drop-rate rose with the screams. Sometimes the ball would go right past my hands and hit me on the head or in the face. It was humiliating. The point is, I wasn't a good baseball player to begin with, but I got worse as people scrutinized me critically. I wilted under mistrust.

YOU SHOULD SEE HOW GREAT I CAN BE

The same kind of thing happens with people like the man I just described. The truth is, I am a sinner. I do have a capacity to be oafish, shallow, and arrogant—a great capacity. But whatever my capacity is, it gets bigger when I am with him. I sink to fulfill what I believe his opinion of me is.

On the other hand, do you know people who, when you are with them, enable you to flourish? I know a few. When I am with them I am wiser, funnier, and smarter. You should see how great I can be when I am with my wife, for instance. To this day, after forty years of marriage, I still feel that I overmarried. I really do. She believes such pleasant fictions about me! And when I am with her, those fictions become nonfictions. She knows all my faults: my oafishness, shallowness, and arrogance. But she nevertheless thinks I am a wonderful husband and father, and a delightfully funny and wise man. *Nevertheless!* What an amazing word of grace it is! Her *Nevertheless!* frees me to say *Nevertheless!* too.

God's love works that way on our humanity. To hear and believe the word of grace he speaks to us is to be freed, by that very event, to become more glorious, more holy, more righteous. To be given "the right," as John puts it in his Gospel, "to become children of God" (John 1:12) is to be given something of the power to begin even to act like a child of God. To know that a holy God sees us wholly through the lens of his Son sets us free to become like his Son. A new identity produces new behavior.

There is more at work here than mere psychology—there is supernatural power. For God's word of acceptance in Christ is a powerful *Word* he speaks to us, Christ himself being that same powerful Word who existed with him from the beginning, who was with God and is God, through whom he created all things, and in whom all things hold together.[8]

The Bible, too, is God's Word. Paul put it vividly and powerfully when he wrote, "All Scripture is God-breathed" (2 Timothy 3:16, NIV). He deliberately linked the language of Genesis 1—the breath God breathed into the first humans— with the breath of God in Scripture. The words of Scripture are filled with the Spirit of God himself and work powerfully to shape us into his image, the same way Adam and Eve were formed in the image of God. To meditate on Scripture is to enter into a profound process of personal transformation. God's Word is more than a mere sound or an idea; it is God himself going out and doing what the Word says. When God speaks, his Word creates the reality he speaks. He says, "Let there be light" (Genesis 1:3), and there is light. His word goes out from his mouth and accomplishes what he desires.[9] To hear God say, "You are forgiven" is to be forgiven and changed. "The message is very close at hand," wrote Paul. "It is on your lips and in your heart. And that message is the very message about faith that we preach: If you confess with your mouth that Jesus is Lord and believe in your heart that God raised him from the dead, you will be saved" (Romans 10:8-9).

Over the years, in my work as a pastor, I have often looked into people's eyes as I have served them the Blessed Sacrament, or Communion. It is one of the most precious and moving things I get to do in my calling. Sometimes, as I serve the bread and the cup, and repeat the words of Jesus, "Take and eat; this is my body, broken for you. Drink this in my memory, it is my blood, poured out for you," I think I can see in their faces something of their glory to come. After all, in ways I believe no Christian tradition has fully explained successfully, Jesus is offering his life to us in the

> The words of Scripture are filled with the Spirit of God himself and work powerfully to shape us into his image. To meditate on Scripture is to enter into a profound process of personal transformation.

sacrament. He wants to be in us as intimately as food put in the mouth, chewed, swallowed, and digested—to become part of the very molecular structure of our body. Is there not glory unimaginable and joy inexpressible contained in the offer, "Take and eat. . . . Drink this"? He wants for us to be in him, and he in us. And he said, "I have told you these things so that you will be filled with my joy. Yes, your joy will overflow!" (John 15:11).

So what does Jesus really look like? His physical appearance doesn't matter—it's who he is that attracts us to him. And the promise of God is that we may one day look into a mirror and see something of who he is looking back at us.

CHAPTER 10

DISAPPOINTMENT WITH GOD

SCARS FROM AN OLD WOUND

These trials will show that your faith is genuine. It is being tested as fire tests and purifies gold—though your faith is far more precious than mere gold. So when your faith remains strong through many trials, it will bring you much praise and glory and honor on the day when Jesus Christ is revealed to the whole world.
1 PETER 1:7

We pray for silver, but God gives us gold instead.
MARTIN LUTHER

THE SUMMER OF 1969 I had to face the fact that a girl I had loved for five years was not going to care for me the way I cared for her. It was no moral failure on her part, but it was a galling realization for me. I had invested so much hope in our future together that when it became clear to me that there would be no future, I was angry and bitter. At what? At her; at myself for believing in us so much, for being so vulnerable; but at God, mostly. Though I would never have said it out loud, I had believed on a deep level in my soul that if I lived a good life and faithfully obeyed his commandments, he owed me one big favor; not a lot of favors, but one big one. She was the big one. And when God appeared to renege on the tacit agreement I felt we had, I was disappointed and angry. So for the next year and a half I went out and systematically broke the commandments I had formerly kept. I did just about everything my Sunday school teachers had told me would destroy me. I actually gained quite a reputation for being a great guy to be with for a good time. *Wild* and *crazy* were the adjectives, but there was no joy in me. I had fear tattooed on my heart.

A HEART AS FEARFUL AND HARD AS MINE

That was a long time ago, and it has taken me about that long to understand how much I was like a man who, on the surface, appeared to be the opposite of me. Before my personal crisis, we had a lot in common. The Bible says, "He was careful to obey all of the Lord's commandments and regulations." Of course, after the crisis, that would be very, very unlike me. But throughout, his heart was as fearful and as hard as mine.

His name was Zechariah, and his heart was laid bare on the most important day of his life, the day he would enter the Holy of Holies. How appropriate. That's what happens when you get near a holy God, whose Word "exposes our innermost thoughts and desires. . . . Everything is naked and exposed before his eyes" (Hebrews 4:12-13).

Like all male descendants of Aaron, Zechariah was a priest. By now there were so many of them that they were divided into twenty-four groups, with each group assigned to Temple duty two weeks out of each year. Even within each group, there were so many men that those who officiated at the sacrifices were chosen by lot. A descendant of Aaron might go through his entire life and never get to perform this honor. Even more exclusive a group were those chosen to enter the Holy of Holies, the place where the presence of God was said to dwell, the most sacred space in all of Israel. The priest would enter the holy place as the people's representative, stand before the altar, sprinkle incense on the fire, and as the smoke from the incense rose, pray for the people. Outside, the congregation would wait in complete silence. When they saw the smoke rise from inside the Holy of Holies, they would fall on their faces and offer up their prayers and thanksgivings. Then the priest would walk outside to where the congregation was praying and raise his arms to bless them.

So many things were on Zechariah's mind as he stood in the holy place after being selected for this honor by lot. Like any priest standing in this place, his thoughts would have been filled with the hopes and anguish of Israel, and the prayer that God would send his promised Messiah to deliver them from their enemies. That longing was intensified in Zechariah, for Luke's Gospel tells us that when Zechariah entered the Holy of Holies, it was during the reign of Herod, one of the vilest, most corrupt, and murderous rulers Israel had ever known. On top of that, it had been four hundred years since a prophet had spoken in Israel. Zechariah's constant prayer had been what many Jews prayed: "How long, O Lord?"

THE WEIGHT OF PERSONAL TRAGEDY

But Zechariah was also carrying in his soul the weight of his personal tragedy: he and his wife, Elizabeth, were very old, and had been unable to have children. In that culture, at that time, this was seen as a terrible curse, probably punishment for sin. Even the word commonly used for childlessness spoke of emptiness and deprivation—it was *barren*. Elizabeth was barren, it was whispered among her family and neighbors; she was blank and hollow at the very place in her life where it was most important that she be filled and fruitful.

Standing in the Holy of Holies, Zechariah prayed in the Hebrew fashion, his arms raised and his face lifted upward to heaven. When he concluded his prayer, he lowered his arms and his gaze, and he saw, standing at the right side of the altar, an angel! Luke gives no description of what the angel looked like except to say that, whatever it looked like (or was it felt like?), Zechariah's reaction was terror. Before he could run out of the holy place, the angel had to reassure him: "Do not be afraid, Zechariah; your prayer has been heard. Your wife Elizabeth will bear you a son" (Luke 1:13, NIV). Zechariah's hands covered his mouth, and his terror turned to astonishment. *A son*, he thought, *did he say a son for Elizabeth and me?* And before he could ask the angel to repeat himself, the angel went on to tell him that the significance of this son would reach far beyond him and Elizabeth:

You will have great joy and gladness, and many will rejoice at his birth, for he will be great in the eyes of the Lord. He must never touch wine or other alcoholic drinks. He will be filled with the Holy Spirit, even before his birth. And he will turn many Israelites to the Lord their God. He will be a man with the spirit and power of Elijah. He will prepare the people for the coming of the Lord. He will turn the hearts of the fathers to their children, and he will cause those who are rebellious to accept the wisdom of the godly. (vv. 14-17)

Then Zechariah's astonishment turned to incredulity, or something worse. What he heard was just too much for his mind to understand and his heart to receive. He blurted out, "How can I be sure this will happen? I'm an old man now, and my wife is also well along in years" (v. 18).

"How can I be sure?" At first glance, that sounds like an innocent enough question, quite understandable, really. Surely the angel would understand the old man's pain and unbelief. Life had been hard for him; childlessness and the shame that went with it, along with years of unanswered prayer had left him disappointed with God, calloused in his soul, and afraid to risk believing again. The old man suffered scars from an old wound.[1] Anyone with even the slightest compassion would understand why he doubted. Not so, it appears, for the angel Gabriel took a dim view of Zechariah's wounded soul and question. "How can I be sure?" is really "Do you expect me to believe this?"[2]

I am Gabriel! I stand in the very presence of God. It was he who sent me to bring you this good news! But now, since you didn't believe what I said, you will be silent and unable to speak until the child is born. For my words will certainly be fulfilled at the proper time. (vv. 19-20)

In other words, the angel said, "You say you're an old man? I say I am Gabriel, who stands in the presence of God. Which one are you going to believe, the old man or the angel? You want proof? I'll give you proof: I'll shut your mouth for the next nine months. What you said is so wrong, and so arrogant, that you won't be able to say anything else until you think of something better to say. Your punishment will fit your crime." Even though he stood in the holiest place on earth and was told by the angel Gabriel, who stood in an even holier place—the very presence of God—Zechariah still wouldn't believe what he heard.

Contrast Zechariah with Mary, the virgin girl who was told by the same angel, just a few verses later, that she would become the mother of the Son of God. She asked, "But how can this happen? I am a virgin" (v. 34). Mary wasn't asking cynically how she could possibly believe such a thing; she was asking for more information. She wanted to know what to do next, how God would bring this miracle about. She was a virgin, after all; did this mean she needed to get married right away? Her question didn't come from skepticism, but from wonder and obedience. So Gabriel warmly explained to her the miracle of the virgin birth and gave her a glimpse into the mystery of the Incarnation.

A GOOD MAN IN THE WORST SENSE OF THE WORD

So Zechariah's heart was exposed and laid bare on what should have been the happiest day of his life. In all of his moral rectitude, he was what Mark Twain once described as "a good man in the worst sense of the word." Disappointment with God had hardened into callous unbelief.

As I said, I know this man's heart intimately, as well as its dangers: left undisciplined and uninstructed, disappointment with God will corrode the soul. Disappointment is like anger; the occasions for it to rise up are myriad and unavoidable. Both are part of the struggle of this life, the *agon* of fighting the good fight and running the race marked out for us. Its mere existence is not evil; it's what you do with it that matters. The Bible says, "Don't sin by letting anger control you" (Psalm 4:4; Ephesians 4:26).

Left undisciplined and uninstructed, disappointment with God will corrode the soul.

The same is true of disappointment, which can be very close to anger: "Don't sin by letting disappointment take control of you."

WHY NOT ME?

What does one do when paralyzed by the bitterness and fear of past pain and disappointment? The first thing is to recognize and acknowledge its existence, to admit the reason you may be unable—or unwilling, really—to trust God. Name it. There is a power in the naming.

Second, ask God to change your heart. That may be too bold a move, for it's strange how attached we can become to bitterness and fear. Maybe it is the sense of an injustice having been perpetrated, and the indignation and self-righteousness that follow. It is a small step from believing you have a right to feel as you do to clinging to what you feel as though it were a right. If asking God to change you is too hard, then follow the advice of the great preacher F. B. Meyer. He would often encourage his listeners to ask God to make them *willing to be willing*. Frankly, I sometimes have to ask God to make me willing to be made willing to be willing.

> **It is a small step from believing you have a right to feel as you do to clinging to what you feel as though it were a right.**

Third, practice humility in all the seasons of your life: the good and the bad, the gratifying and the disappointing. Cultivate humility in all seasons as you would a tree, whose fruit will nourish you in days of trouble. Daily acknowledge that God is God and you are not. Confess it as sin when you forget it, for he alone grasps the big picture and all the details. Remember also that the world you live in is a fallen world, not at all what God intended it to be, but that he is redeeming the world with perfect wisdom, love, and power. Until God's redeeming work is complete, there will be disappointments, and worse—real heartrending tragedy. Given the world we live in, when something bad happens to you, your question should not be "Why me?" but "Why not me?"

Disappointment with God can be nothing more than narcissistic pride. God's lack of what we call "bedside manner" with the disappointed can be shocking. He never once coddled that archetypical sufferer Job. He stayed stonily silent amid all Job's angry and anguished questions. And when he did finally speak, he called Job out and challenged him with some of his own questions:

> Do you still want to argue with the Almighty?
>   You are God's critic, but do you have the answers? . . .
> Brace yourself like a man,
>   because I have some questions for you,
>   and you must answer them. (Job 40:2, 7)

Before God finished asking him questions, Job was so overwhelmed and humbled by the vastness and majesty of God that he begged him to stop. In the end, God did not answer a single one of Job's questions, but Job was so satisfied by what he saw of God's grandeur and wisdom that he said:

> I had only heard about you before,
>   but now I have seen you with my own eyes.
> I take back everything I said,
>   and I sit in dust and ashes to show my repentance.
>   (Job 42:5-6)

In the end, Job discovered God to be better than he ever dreamed he was before he suffered. So how seriously should we take ourselves when we are disappointed with a God like that? In his kindness and love, God allows it for a while— witness the prayers of the Psalms. But given too much license, it quickly morphs into silly self-indulgence. Humility tempers disappointment by putting it in its place.

Humility tempers disappointment by putting it in its place.

INFIRMITIES TO CURE ENORMITIES

Fourth, choose hope. God has promised that nothing can separate you from his love and that in all things he works for your salvation. Believe it. Affirm and confess it when you are disappointed, even if you don't feel it; and keep on declaring it until you do feel it.

There are two things about hope that can sustain you in disappointment. One is the knowledge that when God says no to you, it is so he can say a greater yes. Luther wrote, "We pray for silver, but God gives us gold instead." The Puritan Richard Sibbes said that God will sometimes heal us, not by healing us in the way we think he should, but by giving us "infirmities to cure enormities."[3] I know a country and western song that thanks God for unanswered prayer. I sing along with it whenever it's played on the radio because I know that had not God ended the romance I so desperately desired all those years ago, I could never have enjoyed the last forty years with the incredible woman he gave me. She has been exactly who I most needed. As for Zechariah, what could have been better than waiting a lifetime for a son like John?

There is another thing about hope that transforms disappointment: the way God uses the suffering of disappointment to refine your soul. More important than the things you long for and don't have, or the things you loved and lost, is the person you are gaining as you wrestle with God about these things. Loss and disappointment can work on your soul like the fire of a forge on metal, heating it up so it's white-hot, consuming its impurities and shaping it into something beautiful. Peter also encourages us to see trials as good fire to refine faith, producing in us great love and joy:

> These trials will show that your faith is genuine. It is being tested as fire tests and purifies gold—though your faith is far more precious than mere gold. So when your faith remains strong through many trials, it will bring you much praise and glory and honor on the day when Jesus Christ is revealed to the whole world. You love him even though you have never seen him. Though you do not see him now, you trust him; and you rejoice with a glorious, inexpressible joy. The reward for trusting him will be the salvation of your souls. (1 Peter 1:7-9)

KEEP LAUGHING

One last thing to combat disappointment: Learn to laugh. Develop a sense of humor. I know it's counterintuitive, but try setting the promises of God alongside your disappointments. You'll appreciate the disparity between the two—and the sheer incongruity between your sadness and God's final word on your sadness. Let God's final word be the punch line in the grand comedy of the gospel. Zechariah would have gotten off a lot easier if he had laughed like Sarah laughed when she heard news from the angels about a pregnancy late in life. "So she laughed silently to herself and said, 'How could a worn-out woman like me enjoy such pleasure, especially when my master—my husband—is also so old?'" (Genesis 18:12).

"Enjoy such pleasure"? Imagine the two old coots looking coyly at each other that night in their tent, Abraham in his hundreds and Sarah in her nineties, and saying, "Well, what do you think, dear?" Pretty funny, I'd say. Why did they laugh? Frederick Buechner has an opinion on the matter:

> They laughed because they knew only a fool would
> believe that a woman with one foot in the grave was
> soon to have her other foot in the maternity ward.
> They laughed because God expected them to believe
> it anyway. They laughed because God seemed to
> believe it. They laughed because they half-believed
> it themselves. They laughed because laughing felt
> better than crying. They laughed because if by some
> crazy chance it happened to come true they would

really have something to laugh about, and in the meanwhile *it helped keep them going.*[4]

Amen, brother Frederick! Take heed and heart, all you who are disappointed with God.

PART 4

THE ESSENTIALS

HOW TO FIGHT THE GOOD FIGHT

YEARS AFTER THAT FIRST CAMPFIRE where I threw a piece of wood into the fire to signify my willingness to follow God anywhere, there was another campfire. This time I was the speaker—or one of the coaches, actually. It was the last evening we would all be together after five weeks of intense spiritual and physical training. We had gathered to declare to each other our purposes and commitments once we left the camp and returned home.

The program was called The Blue Helmets, a leadership, physical fitness, and spiritual formation program for high school boys. Every day we would get up at 5:00 a.m. and run two miles uphill in the high altitude to a lake where we would take a polar bear swim. Then, after completing a series of push-ups and pull-ups, we would run back to our cabins to shower and dress. A full day of hard manual labor, weight training, Bible study, and prayer followed.

As one of the coaches, I did everything the boys did. The regimen was grueling and exhilarating. Deep and lasting friendships were built, and there was always a lot of laughter. Males can do some pretty funny things when they are sweating and tired and pulling together toward a common goal.

Most of the boys in the program were ordinary kids and athletes. But a few were elite athletes, Division 1 college material. Two of these athletes were waiting in line to stand before the fire and pledge before God and their brothers how they would live when they went back to the "real world." Both were varsity football players: big, muscular, smart, good-looking, and as humble as adolescents with such gifts can reasonably be. But both were burdened with guilt and regrets for moral failures the year before. They knew it would be hard to live honorably when they went back to their campuses. Their bodies were strong, but their wills were weak.

The first young man stood at the fire looking down at the ground. He was near tears. With anguish in his voice he said, "I really, really hope I will live differently. Pray for me, brothers." My heart went out to him and then sank. He was already defeated.

The second kid got up and looked squarely at us all. I could see the muscles in his jaws and neck flexing. He was obviously moved by what his friend had just said. His voice was hoarse with emotion, as he said firmly and loudly, "I don't *hope* I will live differently next year. I *will* live differently." He walked straight to his demoralized friend and gave him a bear hug.

I thought the whole group was going to stand up and cheer, but they didn't. And I'm glad they didn't—because both men failed miserably the next year. One said he hoped he would be better but wasn't; the other said he would be better but wasn't either. I eventually lost touch with both guys, so I don't know how the rest of their lives turned out, but I fear that second year of failure might have set up a trajectory of hopelessness in their lives.

I wish I had known then what I know now, so that I could have taught them this truth: the Christian life is a marathon, not a sprint. The question is not whether we will fail at times; it is what we will do when we fail, and before we fail. G. K. Chesterton said famously that Christianity "has not been tried and found wanting. It has been found difficult; and left untried." I would paraphrase that to say, "It has been found difficult and not been *practiced* and *persisted* in."

He who began a good work in you is even more determined than you are to complete it (see Philippians 1:6). With each cycle of failure, forgiveness, and restoration, you will grow stronger—but it will take a long time, a lifetime. Ninety percent of the Christian life is just showing up, again and again and again.

One way we show up is by practicing what the church calls the means of grace. These are ways we can position ourselves to receive God's grace. Jesus said the Spirit is like the wind; there is nothing we can do to control the Spirit. But wise believers have long known that there are ways we can spread our sails to catch the wind. These are the essentials of a faith being made muscular.

CHAPTER 11

PERSISTENT PRAYER

HOLY CHUTZPAH

This woman is driving me crazy. I'm going to see that she gets justice,
because she is wearing me out with her constant requests!
LUKE 18:5

Cast yourself into [God's] arms not to be caressed but to wrestle with him.
He loves that holy war.
P. T. FORSYTH, *THE SOUL OF PRAYER*

"WHY IS IT when we talk to God we call it prayer, but when
God talks to us, we call it schizophrenia?"[1]

Prayer as a monologue or soliloquy doesn't present much
of a problem to the modern mind. What Pascal called the
"gods of the philosophers" seem to make more sense; enti-
ties like Alfred North Whitehead's "principle of concretion";
Henry Nelson Wieman's "integrating factor in experience";
or Paul Tillich's "ground of all being." These gods are abstrac-
tions, objects for contemplation and discussion only, not for
a conversation.

But "the field of second-rate religion is strewn with the
corpses of abstract nouns,"[2] wrote George Buttrick. The
Bible agrees. The great people of prayer—Moses, Jeremiah,
Paul, and a nameless Gentile mother from the region of Tyre

and Sidon—insist that prayer is a dialogue with a personal God, even at times a struggle and a wrestling. In fact, it was this anonymous mom whom Jesus singled out as an exemplar of prayer after she had wrestled with him in prayer.

This had to chagrin his disciples. They had tried to send her away because she was an annoyance, a pain in the neck. "Pain in the neck" is a good expression for someone who, like a stiff, sore neck, will irritate you no matter which way you turn. She wouldn't take no for an answer. She pestered and probed and cajoled until she got what she wanted. And Jesus, the master of prayer, lauded this pain in the neck as a great example of how to pray. That is the way it so often is with God: his ways are not our ways, and what makes us want to stop our ears, opens his. God, it would seem, likes to be pestered.

> **Prayer is a dialogue with a personal God, even at times a struggle and a wrestling.**

A MOM AT PRAYER

Part of what so moved Jesus about this woman's prayer had to have been the fact that she was a mother. Matthew's Gospel[3] says that she approached him when Jesus went north to the region of Tyre and Sidon. "A Gentile woman who lived there came to him, pleading, 'Have mercy on me, O Lord, Son of David! For my daughter is possessed by a demon that torments her severely'" (Matthew 15:22).

She was a mom at prayer, a parent. She was a little bit like

God, our Father in heaven, who bragged to Satan about his servant Job, an exemplary and righteous man, who feared God, shunned evil, and was such a good father that he prayed faithfully for his adult children (see Job 1:5). There is something deep in the character of God that responds to the prayers of parents, and to all who pray the way parents pray. Maybe it's because the prayers of moms and dads can be so very humble and self-effacing, because to be a parent is, almost by definition, to be humbled, even humiliated. All parents are in over their heads; they're amateurs, which is a pretty good word, since it comes from the French *amator*, which means "lover." Good parents do what they do simply for the love of it. Beware of the professionals.

Moments before my first son was born, I was scrubbing up in the hall outside the delivery room, preparing to enter the sanctum sanctorum to be with my wife and meet for the first time our firstborn, this holy little creature from a distant galaxy. I was thrilled and scared. I thought, *Life will never be the same again. There's no turning back.* For the first few days after his birth I almost trembled when I held him, afraid I might drop this precious life. He was so dependent, and I was so inadequate. In the years that followed, as his dependence decreased, my sense of inadequacy increased! Far worse things might happen to him, over which I had even less control. I have a list of what I call the things that have driven me to my knees (in prayer). The first four items on the list are Dan, Joel, Andy, and Mary—the names of my four children. I sometimes tell the college students I minister to: Go easy on your parents. They don't know what they're doing; they're all in over their heads.

This can make parents shameless in their pleading. For the sake of her son, the Shunammite woman threw herself to the earth and clung to the prophet Elijah (see 2 Kings 4:27). The nobleman of Capernaum cried to Jesus, "Lord, please come now before my little boy dies" (John 4:49). Jairus fell at Jesus' feet and begged him to heal his "little daughter" before she died (Mark 5:22-23). The prayers of moms and dads stretch them and their faith to the point of breaking. A desperate father brought his demonized son to Jesus and pleaded not only for his boy, but for his own faith. He cried out, that yes, yes, he believed, but prayed for Jesus to "help me overcome my unbelief!" (Mark 9:24).

SHE PROBED BEHIND THE SILENCE

I think Jesus also loved it that this Gentile woman was not turned back by his silence. When at first she prayed to the Lord, *"Jesus gave her no reply, not even a word,"* neither a yes nor a no (Matthew 15:23, italics mine). The silence of God is the greatest test of our faith. Sometimes it's in places with names like Dachau, Buchenwald, or Pol Pot's Cambodia; or as we look into the terrified eyes of an abused child or the gaunt stare of an AIDS baby. God's silence can be seen in the rows of amputees in a veterans hospital or the mentally tortured in a psychiatric ward. God's silence is felt in the weight of crushing grief, described by C. S. Lewis in *A Grief Observed*:

Meanwhile, where is God? . . . When you are happy, so happy that you have no sense of needing Him, so happy that you are tempted to feel His claims upon you as an interruption, if you remember yourself and turn to Him with gratitude and praise, you will be—or so it feels—welcomed with open arms. But go to Him when your need is desperate, when all other help is vain, and what do you find? A door slammed in your face, and a sound of bolting and double bolting on the inside. After that, silence. You may as well turn away. The longer you wait, the more emphatic the silence will become. There are no lights in the windows. It might be an empty house. Was it ever inhabited? It seemed so once. And that seeming was as strong as this. What can this mean? Why is He so present a commander in our time of prosperity and so very absent a help in time of trouble?[4]

God can be silent when people aren't. The disciples weren't silent; they had plenty to say. They wanted to be done with her: "'Tell her to go away,' they said. 'She is bothering us with all her begging'" (v. 23).

The silence of God is the greatest test of our faith.

But nevertheless the woman clung to the silent Jesus because she sensed that the silence of God was to be measured by other standards than human silence. She groped and probed behind the silence, because the silence of Jesus is not the silence of indifference; it is the silence of higher thoughts.[5] It's the silence of Jesus deep asleep in the boat as a storm raged around his disciples and threatened to sink the boat. Even nature spoke, but he didn't. And the Cross, God's greatest silence, was the silence of his greatest and deepest thoughts. So the woman persisted in spite of the silence.

SHE'S UNDAUNTED BY PERPLEXITY

And when Jesus finally spoke, what she heard was worse than what she hadn't heard. "Then Jesus said to the woman, 'I was sent only to help God's lost sheep—the people of Israel'" (v. 24). In other words, he said to her, "You're not on my agenda. I have higher priorities than you and your little girl." Those words would have crushed me. I would have walked away shaking my head, wondering, *What kind of God is this?* But instead of walking away, she pressed her case. He might have said awful things she couldn't understand, but she was convinced that he could help her and that was all that mattered. Undeterred, *"she came and worshiped him, pleading again, 'Lord, help me!'"* (v. 25, italics mine). And when she did, things got even worse! "Jesus responded, 'It isn't right to take food from the children and throw it to the dogs'" (v. 26).

It doesn't take an expert in biblical interpretation to see that Jesus added insult to injury: the children equal Israel; the dogs equal the Gentiles, *her*. Not only is she excluded from his circle of concern; she is included in his circle of contempt. Or so it seems. Once again, he had said awful things she couldn't understand, worse things! But she remained convinced that Jesus could help her, so she pressed in, "That's true, Lord, but even dogs are allowed to eat the scraps that fall beneath their masters' table" (v. 27).

Far from taking personal offense at this deliberate rebuff, the woman gracefully turned the last shred of her pride into a burnt offering for her suffering daughter. And Jesus answered her, "Dear woman . . . your faith is great. Your request is granted" (v. 28). Her daughter was instantly healed.

Sometimes Jesus doesn't talk the way one might expect the Son of a compassionate God to talk. He can sound pretty harsh. He can seem as mean as the title of Mark Galli's fine little book: *Jesus, Mean and Wild*. There are plausible explanations by Bible commentators for why Jesus spoke to her the way he did, all of which try to demonstrate why he probably wasn't really as nasty and curmudgeonly as he sounded. With a little cultural context and a closer reading, they show how Jesus comes out sounding much nicer. I have no fundamental argument with these interpretations. But I also think we should let his words stand as the difficult thing they are. The point of his brusque language, it seems to me, is that God is often a perplexing God, and if we're not prepared to wrestle with perplexity, we aren't prepared to persevere in prayer to this God. God is not, as philosopher Peter Kreeft wrote, "a hard, bright, brittle, little formula but a mystery. He is the God of whom Rabbi Abraham Heschel said, 'God is not nice. God is not an uncle. God is an earthquake.'"[6]

SHE'S LOADED WITH CHUTZPAH

The woman seems to know this about God. There is so much she can't understand about him, but she is absolutely clear about one thing: God is her only hope, and she won't let go of her only hope until she gets what she needs. Her faith is not the capacity for a comprehensive and nuanced theology, or for mystical experience and flights of religious ecstasy. Her faith is the raw, relentless trust that Jesus can help her, and the dogged determination to keep going to him until he does.

The lady is loaded with *chutzpah*—a Yiddish word difficult to define with a single English word. It means something like headstrong persistence, brazen impudence, unyielding tenacity, bold determination, raw nerve, even gall. In his parables on prayer, Jesus loved to portray faith as *chutzpah*: as a friend banging on a sleeping neighbor's door at midnight, waking up a whole village, in order to shame him into providing the food he needed for his guest; or a widow badgering a corrupt judge for justice he does not want to give her, until he relents, throws up his hands, and growls, "This woman is driving me crazy. I'm going to see that she gets justice, because she is wearing me out with her constant requests!" Both are pains in the neck![7]

Chutzpah is the Gentile woman's essential quality, which makes all the others possible. *Chutzpah* is another word for faith. It was in reference to the pain-in-the-neck widow who drove the corrupt judge crazy that Jesus said, "When the Son of Man returns, how many will he find on the earth *who have faith?*" (Luke 18:8, italics mine).

P. T. Forsyth, the great theologian of prayer, hated resignation and fatalism in prayer. He believed that sometimes to resist the will of God is to do the will of God, if what we resist is what God wills to be temporary and intermediary— poor health, a bad job, a difficult marriage, or *a demonized daughter*, for instance. It may be God's will that you be in these circumstances now, but not that you stay in them: "He has a lower will and a higher, a prior and a posterior. And the purpose of the lower will is that it be resisted and struggled through to the higher."[8] Wrestling in prayer from the lower to the higher is one of God's chief means of educating our spirits.

> Resist God, in the sense of rejecting God, and you
> will not be able to resist any evil. But resist God in
> the sense of closing with God, cling to him with all
> your strength, not your weakness only, with your
> active and not only your passive faith, and he will
> give you strength. Cast yourself into his arms not to
> be caressed but to wrestle with him. He loves that
> holy war. He may be too many for you, and lift you
> from your feet. But it will be to lift you from earth,
> and set you in the heavenly places which are theirs
> who fight the good fight and lay hold of God as their
> eternal life.[9]

To pray with *chutzpah* is to pray with the same *agon*, the same fierce determination and focus that Jesus said was necessary to enter his Kingdom. When Luther watched his dog waiting for a bone, furiously wagging his tail, eyes gleaming with anticipation, he said, "If only I would pray that way." That's *chutzpah*. Armin Gesswein said prayer was simply pleading the promises of God, insisting that God do the kinds of things he said he would do, and not stopping until he does. That's *chutzpah*. It may also have been Luther who said prayer is throwing the bag of God's promises at his feet and delighting to discover that it's so big he can't step over it! That's *chutzpah*! And God loves it.

CHAPTER 12

PATIENT PRAYER

THE HAMMER STROKES OF PRAYER

We also pray that you will be strengthened with all his glorious power so you will have all the endurance and patience you need.
COLOSSIANS 1:11

Our prayers are hammer-strokes against the bulwarks of the princes of darkness; they must be oft repeated. Many years can pass by, even a number of generations die away, before a breakthrough occurs. However, not a single hit is wasted; and if they are continued, then even the most secure wall must finally fall.
J. C. AND C. F. BLUMHARDT

FILL IN THE BLANK: "If I could be strengthened with all of God's glorious power, I would use it to: _____."

Think of all the great things you could do if you had all of God's glorious power. You could heal the sick and end world hunger, find a cure for AIDS and raise the dead, transform the culture and stop human trafficking. And you'd just be getting started.

The way the apostle Paul filled in the blank is surprising. He told the Colossian Christians he was praying that they would be strengthened with all God's glorious power "so you will have all the endurance and patience you need" (Colossians 1:11). What? He didn't pray that they would be strengthened to do great acts of power, but just to hang in and tough it out, to be patient and endure. You might think, *What a waste of power*—if you've never had to be patient and endure something really hard, that is. It's hard to endure and

Patient endurance *is* a great act of power.

be patient; so hard, in fact, that only God's power can make it possible. Waiting in the midst of frustration and suffering is one

of the hardest things any of us will ever have to do. Patient endurance *is* a great act of power.

One big reason for this is that God can be so very hard to work with—mainly because his sense of time is so very different from ours. A thousand years for him are "as a passing day, as brief as a few night hours" (Psalm 90:4). One almost always has to wait longer than seems reasonable to us humans for God to do whatever he is doing. Don't ask me why; that's just the way God is.

At the entrance of the fossil museum beside the La Brea tar pits in Los Angeles, there once was a painting of a long ribbon, representing scientists' view of 5 billion years of the earth's history. The ribbon was eighty-five feet long, one inch equaling 5 million years. Guess how much space on that ribbon belonged to the history of the human race, from the cavemen to the astronauts—less than one-half inch. When I saw that ribbon for the first time, I just stared and gawked, wondering what God would have been doing the other 84 feet, 11½ inches. The time of those weird creatures we call the dinosaurs lasted 100 million years alone. Assuming the scientists' estimate of this period was on target, what was that about? God only knows, and he's not talking; that's just the way he does things, and to get connected with God's grand purposes for his creation is inevitably to get frustrated with the way he takes his own sweet time. You'll need some of God's glorious and great power to patiently endure as you wait for him.

HAMMER STROKES OF PRAYER

Nowhere is this more evident than in prayer. I love to hear stories about instant answers to prayer, and I can tell a few of my own. But the truth is most answers to prayer come at the end of long periods of "waiting on the Lord," trusting that he has heard us and is accomplishing his good work in the way and the time that he, in his wisdom and power, deems best. But that's hard to do, and I have often had to turn to the pastoral wisdom of two nineteenth-century German pastors, J. C. and C. F. Blumhardt, a father and a son, for encouragement. They wrote:

> Our prayers are hammer-strokes against the bulwarks of the princes of darkness; they must be oft repeated. Many years can pass by, even a number of generations die away, before a breakthrough occurs. However, not a single hit is wasted; and if they are continued, then even the most secure wall must finally fall. Then the glory of God will have a clear path upon which to stride forth with healing and blessing for the wasted fields of mankind.

George Muller, another great nineteenth-century man of prayer, knew about the oft-repeated hammer-strokes of persevering prayer. He recorded in his diary how in November 1844, he began to pray for the conversion of five young men:

I prayed every day without a single intermission, whether sick or in health, on the land or on the sea, and whatever the pressure of my engagements might be. Eighteen months elapsed before the first of the five was converted. I thanked God and prayed on for the others. Five years elapsed, and then the second was converted. I thanked God for the second, and prayed on for the other three. Day by day, I continued to pray for them, and six years passed before the third was converted. I thanked God for the three, and went on praying for the other two. These two remained unconverted.[1]

Another thirty-six years passed, and Muller still could not report the conversion of these last two holdouts. But he remained confident and wrote, "But I hope in God, I pray on, and look yet for the answer. They are not converted yet, *but they will be*."[2] It wasn't until after Muller died, fifty-two years after he began to pray for these two men, that they were finally converted. Muller went to his death still not having seen the answer to his prayers but obeying the Lord's command to "always pray and never give up" (Luke 18:1). He stood with other heroes of faith who suffered and persevered and died, though "none of them received all that God had promised" (Hebrews 11:39). He knew God's pledge to answer prayer would not be canceled just because he died.

MUSTARD SEED PRAYERS

Jesus said the Kingdom of God is like the tiniest of seeds, a mustard seed, planted in the soil. That seed disappears and "dies" and then sprouts forth with new life when its time has come. It starts small, but with perseverance it grows into a huge plant (see Luke 13:18-19).

In the winter of 1628, almost two hundred years before Muller, Jan Amos Comenius and a ragtag bunch of his church members knelt in the snow at the Polish border and prayed a wistful but bold mustard seed prayer. Caught in the turmoil of Catholic-Protestant rivalry of the Thirty Years War, they had been forced to leave their beloved Bohemia. They knelt shivering, and as they looked back longingly at their homeland, Comenius asked God to preserve in Bohemia "a hidden seed to glorify thy name," an appropriate metaphor for a winter prayer. But Comenius never saw his prayer answered—forty-two years later, in 1670, he died an expatriate, penniless and homeless. He did, however, leave the world 154 books that were seminal in the formation of modern ideas about Christian education.

His prayer was answered one hundred years later when young Count Nikolaus von Zinzendorf opened his family estate in Moravia as a refuge for the followers of Comenius.

They called their community the *Herrnhut,* or "Lord's Watch" in German. Since they themselves were the fruit of a mustard seed prayer, they took their name from Isaiah 62:6-7, a great text on mustard seed prayer:

> *I have posted watchmen on your walls, Jerusalem;*
>   *they will never be silent day or night.*
> *You who call on the LORD,*
>   *give yourselves no rest,*
> *and give him no rest till he establishes Jerusalem*
>   *and makes her the praise of the earth.* (NIV)

The Moravian Brethren, as they came to be known, were the pioneers of modern missions. In the first one hundred years of their existence, they maintained a continuous twenty-four-hour, seven-days-a-week prayer vigil and sent two thousand missionaries to the ends of the earth. It was at a Moravian prayer meeting in London that John Wesley felt his heart "strangely warmed." From that encounter came the world-shaking Wesleyan revival, the impact of which we feel to this day.

Comenius prayed for God to preserve in Bohemia "a hidden seed to glorify thy name." From a human perspective, it seemed that God did nothing for a century. But for the next two and a half centuries he went far beyond anything that little bunch of refugees could have ever imagined—beyond Bohemia to the world!

God's ways are not our ways. His timing is not our

timing. Where are you in your prayers now? Kneeling with Comenius in the snow? Wondering with Comenius at the end of his life?

One of the most remarkable passages in all Scripture about persevering prayer shows the martyred saints in heaven still hammering against the bulwarks of the princes of darkness, still praying for the justice they were denied: "O Sovereign Lord, holy and true, how long before you judge the people who belong to this world and avenge our blood for what they have done to us?" (Revelation 6:10).

Even in heaven, these brave and persistent saints are crying out for the Kingdom to come. And it also appears that even in heaven they still need to be strengthened to persevere, for "a white robe was given to each of them. And they were told to rest a little longer until the full number of their brothers and sisters—their fellow servants of Jesus who were to be martyred—had joined them" (v. 11).

PRAYER AS THERMOMETER AND THERMOSTAT

As important as prayer is to Jesus, it's significant that he actually said so little about how to pray. The content of prayer is clear—all summed up in the Lord's Prayer, the "Our Father." Beyond that, Jesus recommends no techniques; all he urges is persistence and perseverance. I'm not sure why, but my guess—no, my strong conviction—is that Jesus sees prayer as both a thermometer and a thermostat of the Christian life. Thermometers register the temperature in a room; thermostats regulate the temperature. Thermometers tell you what is; thermostats change what is. As a thermometer, the quality of our prayers is an indicator of the quality of our whole lives. Persevering people pray persevering prayers. What they do in the world, they also do before God. Moreover, as a thermostat, the quality of our prayers will affect the quality of what we do in the world. People who persevere in prayer will begin to persevere in other things.

The point is, there is an indissoluble link between prayer and action, praying and doing. All genuine Christian action begins with prayer because all genuine Christian action begins with God. Prayer is central because God is central, and prayer is central in the same way the hub is central in a wheel; there is more to a wheel than a hub—there are spokes and a rim—but without the hub the rest of the wheel is pretty useless.

All genuine Christian action begins with prayer because all genuine Christian action begins with God.

There is more to do than pray, but you won't get to it until you pray. Or as A. J. Gordon wrote, "You can do more than pray after you have prayed; but you can never do more than pray until you have prayed."

Now couple the intimate relationship between work and prayer with God's penchant for doing his great work over time, usually long periods of time, like the farmer's work to which Jesus compared the Kingdom. When you do this, Paul's prayer for the Colossians makes more sense: "We also pray that you will be strengthened with all his glorious power

so you will have all the endurance and patience you need"
(Colossians 1:11).

We've got to hang in with the work and the prayer, the
way a marathon runner hangs in with the running. The
Christian's *agon* is to "run with endurance the race God has
set before us . . . keeping our eyes on Jesus, the champion
who initiates and perfects our faith" (Hebrews 12:1-2). It
takes the mighty power of Christ to do this. None of us is
capable of this in our own strength.

HARDER WORK THAN DOING

Mary Slessor was an indefatigable worker—she had to be,
for her work was rescuing orphans in West Africa. And she
was very busy; no one is busier than a mom with a bunch of
little kids, and Slessor was a "mom" to many, with very little
help. Yet she credited prayer as the source of her strength to
endure. Prayer was the thermometer and the thermostat for
her work. It was praying and doing, doing and praying that
unified and energized her life. In letters home to her friends
she wrote:

> My life is one long daily, hourly, record of answered
> prayer. For physical health, for mental overstrain, for
> guidance given marvelously, for errors and dangers
> averted, for enmity to the Gospel subdued, for food
> provided at the exact hour needed, for everything
> that goes to make up life and my poor service, I can

testify with a full and often wonder-stricken awe
that I . . . know God answers prayer. . . . Prayer is
the greatest power God has put into our hands for
service. Praying is harder work than doing . . . but
the dynamic lies that way to advance the Kingdom.
. . . Pray on—power lies that way.[3]

Not many of us are Slessors, Mullers, or Comeniuses. But
the differences between them and the rest of us is not in kind
but in degree. Like them, we all have plenty to do, hard things,
the doing of which won't be done unless we have the strength
to endure. And like them, we must repent of the conceit and
delusion that we can handle things in our own strength.

Prayer is not something to be incorporated into our busy
lives or thrown on top of the pile of obligations that dominates our days. Rather, prayer must rearrange and even delete
some of our obligations. If
we believe that "prayer is the
greatest power God has put
into our hands for service,"
then we will start with prayer,
and with whatever time is left
over after we pray, we do the
other things. "Our true aim," wrote Andrew Murray, "must
not be to work a great deal and pray just enough to keep
the work right. We should pray a great deal and then work
enough for the power and blessing obtained in prayer to find
its way through us to men."[4]

> Prayer is not something to be incorporated into our busy lives; rather, prayer must rearrange and even delete some of our obligations.

Marriage can be long, arduous work, the raising of children more than some can endure. Those who care for the
handicapped and aged, for the mentally ill and the terminally
ill, need patient endurance. Then there are the *agonistes* of
the workaday world: blessed are those whose work is fulfilling, but common are those who say of their work what Studs
Terkel concluded in his bestseller *Working*:

> This book, being about work, is, by its very nature,
> about violence—to the spirit as well as to the
> body. It is about ulcers as well as accidents, about
> shouting matches as well as fistfights, about nervous
> breakdowns as well as kicking the dog around. It is,
> above all (or beneath all), about daily humiliations.
> To survive the day is triumph enough for the
> walking wounded among the great many of us.[5]

Beyond the ordinary struggles of daily living, there are the
great intractable evils—sin, death, and misery—we would
like to defeat through God's glorious power. Only God can
defeat them, but it pleases him to make us his Kingdom
partners and call us into his great work of restoration, justice,
and healing in the world. We pray not only that he will do
what we cannot, but that what we cannot do, we can do with
him, by patient endurance. It will take time, a lot of time; it
already has been two thousand years since Christ "suffered
under Pontius Pilate, was crucified, died, and was buried . . .
rose again from the dead . . . ascended into heaven and sits at

the right hand of God the Father Almighty."[6] No one knows how much more time it will take until he comes again "to judge the living and the dead," but we know it may very well take more time than we have the strength for.

Missionary William Carey is famous for saying, "Expect great things from God, attempt great things for God." It's a good saying, a heroic saying, inspiring and true. Not so well known was what he said to his father when he was a young man. When he announced to his family that God had called him to be a missionary in India, his father did everything he could to dissuade him from that venture, mainly by reminding Carey of all his weaknesses and handicaps. After this systematic dismantling of his self-esteem, Carey said quietly and firmly to his father, "I can plod." And plod he did, expecting great things from God and attempting great things for God.

So we pray for patient endurance, and we pray with patient endurance.

CHAPTER 13

JOY

THE HEART OF A FIGHTER

Always be joyful. Never stop praying. Be thankful in all circumstances, for
this is God's will for you who belong to Christ Jesus.
1 THESSALONIANS 5:16-18

Would you know who is the greatest saint in the world? It is not he who
prays most or fasts most; it is not he who gives most alms, or is most
eminent for temperance, chastity, or justice; but it is he who is always
thankful to God, who wills everything that God willeth, who receives
everything as an instance of God's goodness, and has a heart always ready
to praise God for it. . . . Could you therefore work miracles, you could not
do more for yourself, than by this thankful spirit, for it . . . turns all that it
touches into happiness.
WILLIAM LAW, *DEVOUT AND HOLY LIFE*

IT'S HARD TO be a Christian—to run the way Jesus did and
fight the good fight the way he fought the good fight. As if
that weren't hard enough, we're told to fight the good fight
with joy, of all things: "And let us run with endurance the
race God has set before us. We do this by keeping our eyes
on Jesus, the champion who initiates and perfects our faith.
Because of the *joy* awaiting him, he endured the cross, disregarding its shame" (Hebrews 12:1-2, italics mine).

I had always thought endurance was something one does
with clenched fists and teeth. Now consider this: Are we

supposed to clench our teeth and be joyful too? It has taken me most of my life to get this, but what I was missing in the equation is that joy is not an additional requirement for the good fight but the very thing that makes fighting the good fight possible. Joy is a powerful weapon in the good fight—it's what kept Jesus going in his good fight.

Joy is not an additional requirement for the good fight but the very thing that makes fighting the good fight possible.

Here is a picture of how joy works in the good fight. The church I pastored in New Jersey funded the translation of the *JESUS* film into the language of a primitive people group in the jungles of East Asia. The account I heard of the premier of the film among these people is itself a reason for joy. Keep in mind that they had never heard of Jesus and never seen a motion picture. Imagine the mystery and delight of seeing and hearing the story of Jesus for the first time, almost like an eyewitness. Imagine how you would feel when you saw this good man who healed sick people and was adored by children suddenly arrested, held without trial, and beaten by jeering soldiers.

The people came unglued. They began to shout and shake their fists at the men on the screen. When nothing happened, they turned their ire toward the missionary running the projector. Maybe he was the one responsible for this injustice! He had to stop the film to explain that there was more to come, that the story wasn't over yet. So they reluctantly regained their composure and settled down to watch what happened next.

What came next was the Crucifixion. Again the people came apart. They threw themselves on the ground and wept and wailed. There was so much noise, the missionary stopped the film once more to explain that the story wasn't finished. Again they composed themselves.

Then came the Resurrection. The missionary had to stop the film again, this time not because of the people's anger but because of the celebration that erupted among them! A party broke out spontaneously with dancing and singing and back-slapping, because *joy is what you experience when you are grateful for the grace that has been given you.* Indeed, if one could ever truly take to heart the goodness and generosity of God—really see it in its height, depth, width, and length[1]—one might act just like the people in that village. If our gratitude could perfectly correspond to the grace that is given us, then no amount of thanksgiving and joy could possibly be excessive.

Grace is God's mercy, his unearned favor. Grace is what Frederick Buechner calls the gospel's "crucial eccentricity," the unique and wonderfully odd thing God does to forgive sinners, not giving them the bad things they do deserve but the incredibly good things they don't deserve. The great gospel mystery is not that bad things sometimes happen to good people but that such a good and gracious thing has happened to bad people, guilty and broken people, who have discovered God's amazing love to be just that—amazing. "God

> Joy is what you experience when you are grateful for the grace that has been given you.

showed his great love for us by sending Christ to die for us while we were still sinners" (Romans 5:8). Real Christians have been known to get ecstatic over this.

THE PULSE OF THE FIGHTER

What else can one be but profoundly grateful when grace like that happens? "How can anything more or different be asked of man?" asks Karl Barth. "Grace and gratitude belong together like heaven and earth. Grace evokes gratitude like the voice of an echo. Gratitude follows grace like thunder lightning."[2] Barth's words paint a lively picture; God looks into the abyss, the Grand Canyon, of human guilt and sin and shouts, "Grace!" The echo comes back exuberantly, "Thank you, thank you, thank you, thank you," from every direction.

> **Grace is like a blinding flash of lightning, splitting the sky on a dark night. Gratitude is the thundering response.**

Grace is like a blinding flash of lightning, splitting the sky on a dark night. Gratitude is the thundering response.

Grace, gratitude, and joy are joined organically, theologically, and spiritually. In the Greek language, they are even related linguistically. The words for grace, gratitude, and joy all have the same root, *char*, a noun that refers to health and well-being. Grace is *charis*, gratitude is *eucharistia*, and joy is *chara*. It is a picture of the burning reality of the Christian gospel.

The French philosopher and Jesuit priest Pierre Teilhard

de Chardin wrote, "Joy is the most infallible sign of the presence of God." Conversely, the absence of joy, because it signals the absence of gratitude, is the most infallible sign of the absence of God and of the presence of the nominal religion I've been railing against. How else are we to understand the latecomers in Jesus' parable of the no-shows, the complacent and the mildly interested, the slackers and the unimpressed, the unfazed and the unmoved (see Matthew 22:1-10)—except as monumentally ungrateful?

To run and fight and endure like Jesus, because of joy, is to be grateful. Grateful for what? For the mercy and grace of God that not only called us out of darkness into light but also into his service. To use Barth's image, gratitude—and therefore joy—is the thunder of the Christian's fight. Poet George Herbert liked the picture of a heart's pulse. He asked God to make him grateful in all circumstances, happy or sad:

> Not thankful when it pleaseth me,
> As if Thy blessings had spare dayes;
> But such a heart whose pulse may be
>   Thy praise.[3]

Let gratitude pump through my soul the way blood pumps through my body! For I die without either. In praise, notes Theodore Jennings, "God's mirth roars in our veins and we are alive and enlivened." God's Spirit moves like oxygen in the bloodstream of our souls.

So the Christian athlete (and every Christian is a spiritual athlete, or no Christian at all) must cultivate gratitude the way a runner strengthens his heart: by constant, daily practice and repetition. I think that is why the Bible commands an almost indiscriminate gratefulness. Gratitude and joy are organs of perception. We don't see in order to give thanks and rejoice; we give thanks and rejoice in order to see. Do you see no reason to be joyful and grateful? Rejoice and give thanks so you will! For the truth of our human limitations is that we never see all there is to see, whether of evil or good. We never have all the information. Our perceptions are radically the result of our dispositions.

The Christian must cultivate gratitude the way a runner strengthens his heart: by constant, daily practice and repetition.

But if God is all he claims to be in Scripture, if he indeed is always working in all things "for the good of those who love God and are called according to his purpose for them" (Romans 8:28), then we have every reason to be disposed toward gratitude even when all our eyes can see looks terrible. How could anything be more pleasing to the God who cannot be pleased without faith (Hebrews 11:6) than to exercise faith and rejoice and give thanks anyway, regardless of circumstances? To exercise the discipline of thanksgiving is to thank God for what you see, and when you can see nothing to thank him for, then thank him for what you do not see.

So when thieves robbed Matthew Henry, the great eighteenth-century Bible scholar, he wrote in his diary, "Let me be thankful first because I was never robbed before;

second, although they took my purse, they did not take my life; third, because, although they took my all, it was not much; and fourth, because it was I who was robbed, and not someone else." It's hard to know what to make of this outlook.

Henry's outlook was not unique to him. William Law, another eighteenth-century Christian thinker, took the same position. He believed thankfulness works miracles and "turns all that it touches into happiness." For Law, the greatest saint "is not he who prays most or fasts most; it is not he who gives most alms, or is most eminent for temperance, chastity, or justice; but it is he who is always thankful to God, who wills everything that God willeth, who receives everything as an instance of God's goodness, and has a heart always ready to praise God for it."[4]

Both Henry and Law were strongly intent on obeying, to the literal letter, the command in Scripture to be indiscriminately thankful—to "rejoice in the Lord always" (Philippians 4:4, NIV). Virginia Owens writes:

For if you go poking about the world, intent
on keeping the candle of consciousness blazing,
you must be ready to give thanks at all times.
Discrimination is not allowed. The flame cannot
gutter and fail when a cold wind whistles throughout
the house. Thanksgiving, thanksgiving. All must
be thanksgiving. . . . Thanksgiving is not a task
to be taken lightly. It is not for dilettantes or

aesthetes. One does not dabble in praise for one's own amusement, nor train the intellect and develop perceptual skills to add to his repertoire. We are not thinking about the world as a free course in art appreciation. No. Thanksgiving is not the result of perception; thanksgiving is the access to perception.[5]

There is a Russian proverb, "Nothing ages faster than gratitude." Thankfulness is not a constant, like your eye color or the shape of your nose. It's like a fire that will go out if not tended to or a garden that will grow fallow if not cultivated. Mostly, it is a memory that will disappear if not refreshed continually. If we do not, we will cease to be amazed and strengthened by grace.

NO LONGER AMAZED BY GRACE

We will become like the students in a class R. C. Sproul taught his first year as a professor. There were 250 first-year students in the class. He informed them that the class assignments included three papers, the first due September 30, the second October 30, and the third November 30. He emphasized that each of the papers must be turned in no later than noon of the due date. An F grade would be given to any late papers, no exceptions. "Does everybody understand the assignment?" he asked. They all said, "Oh, yes."

On September 30, 25 of the 250 students didn't have their papers ready. They begged for mercy from Dr. Sproul, for an extension, for just a little more time, please, please, please. They were, he said, "in a posture of abject humility," pleading for grace. And he gave grace, but with the warning, "Don't let it happen again. Remember the next assignment is due October 30, and I want those papers in." They promised, absolutely, yes.

October 30 came, and this time there were 50 students without papers. They stood outside in terror. Really, they didn't budget their time well; it was midterms and home-coming, and they were swamped. Please, please, please—one more chance, please. Sproul yielded to their entreaties, but with another warning: "Don't let it happen again."

It did. On November 30, 100 students came casually into class minus their papers. They weren't worried in the least. They told Professor Sproul to chill out, not to worry about it, that they'd get their papers in to him in a couple of days. Sproul took out his little black grading book and his pen and asked a student, "Johnson, where's your term paper?" Johnson said he didn't have it, so Sproul wrote an F grade in the book.

He asked another student the same question: "Greenwood, where's your paper?" He didn't have it either. So Sproul wrote another F in the book.

The class was furious! As one person, they shouted, "That's not fair."

Sproul bristled. He said, "Johnson, did I just hear you say that's not fair?"

Johnson came back at him: "Yes, that's not fair."

Sproul answered, "Okay, I don't ever want to be thought of as being unfair or unjust. Johnson, it's justice that you want?" Johnson said yes.

"Okay," said Sproul, "if I recall, you were late the last time, weren't you?" He said yes.

"Okay, I'll go back and change that grade to an F." He erased his passing grade and gave him an F. Then he looked at the class and asked, "Is there anybody else who wants justice?" There were no takers.[6]

The first time the students asked for mercy they asked with a deep sense of what was at stake. They were sober, humble, and grateful when they received it. The next time they just argued their case—a pretty good one it seemed, what with midterms and homecoming and all. It was only fair that they be cut some slack. The third time they didn't look for mercy; they demanded their rights. Their premise had moved from the professor's mercy to the professor's obligation. When gratitude departs, grace disappears, and entitlement quickly takes its place.

When gratitude departs, grace disappears, and entitlement quickly takes its place.

CULTIVATE YOUR MEMORY!

There is an urgency in the Scriptures to remember, for when memory goes so do gratitude and joy. To forget what to be thankful for is to forget why to be joyful. David even talks to himself about it: "Let all that I am praise the LORD; may I never forget the good things he does for me." What is it he is urging himself never to forget? Plenty, and as David reminds himself to remember, only the very dull or nearly dead could not be moved to deep thankfulness and joy at the memory of things like these:

> *He forgives all my sins*
>   *and heals all my diseases.*
> *He redeems me from death*
>   *and crowns me with love and tender mercies.*
> *He fills my life with good things.*
>   *My youth is renewed like the eagle's!* (Psalm 103:3-5)

The cultivation of the memory was important to Jesus, too. He told us to eat a meal, to break the bread and to drink the wine, "in remembrance of me" (Luke 22:19, NIV; see also 1 Corinthians 11:23-26). At the heart of Christian worship is a meal for the stimulation of the memory. We remember two things: our great sinfulness and misery, and the price Christ's great love paid on the Cross to forgive and save us. Our misery is measured by the Cross; our gratitude and joy should be too.

What do we lose when we lose the memory of these things? We forget why we should be joyful. We grow accustomed to his grace. It ceases to be the heart-stopping miracle it is and degenerates into an entitlement, a "right," merely a pleasant feature on the religious landscape. We slide into nominal Christianity.

For God's sake and our own, we must not forget to remember what Os Guinness calls "the once and might have been"[7]—our wretchedness before God's grace and our blessedness with God's grace, which therefore moves us to heartily and humbly say thank you for such amazing grace. Gratitude must follow grace like thunder follows lightning. Praise must be the very heart of the fighter of the good fight.

One of the great images in the Bible of the Christian warrior is of the Messiah, kneeling beside a stream of water in the heat of battle to refresh himself:

> *But he himself will be refreshed from brooks along the way.*
> *He will be victorious.* (Psalm 110:7)

To praise and thank God is to be refreshed. And this refreshment is so near; as near as the prayer of Psalm 51:

> *Unseal my lips, O Lord,*
> *that my mouth may praise you.* (v. 15)

It's as near as the fresh water of the Amazon was to the early European explorers who drifted into the mouth of this great river. The Amazon is the world's biggest river, its volume exceeding the Yangtze, Mississippi, and Nile rivers combined. Its current can be felt two hundred miles into the Atlantic Ocean. Ships caught in the doldrums would sometimes drift into its mouth unknowingly, because its mouth is ninety miles wide. The sailors would be dying of thirst, longing for a drink of fresh water. Natives canoeing out to the ships would be met with frantic cries for fresh water. The natives would laugh and point down to the very water they were sitting in. All that was required was to lower a bucket.

CHAPTER 14

HOPE

THE MELODY OF THE FUTURE

Because of the joy awaiting him, he endured the cross, disregarding
its shame.
HEBREWS 12:2

Hope is hearing the melody of the future. Faith is to dance to it.
RUBEM ALVES

IT WASN'T AN ideal location for a 10K race, or for any kind
of physical exertion, but my friend Ralph and I thought we
would give it a try anyway. It would be held at a scrubby
little park in Pico Rivera, California, which was situated at
the junction of three freeways. That meant the air could be
foul with the toxic gases belched from the thousands of auto-
mobiles and giant semis that would be driving by as we competed. The saving grace, or so we thought, was that the race
would begin early on a Saturday, at 7:00 a.m., when traffic
was sparse and the temperature cool.

We and the other three hundred–plus contestants were
ready to go at 6:45, but the race officials weren't. Fifteen
minutes passed, then thirty, then forty-five, as we all stood
around chatting and stretching—and nervously watching the
sun rise higher and the air get thicker. I was already thirsty

and sweating when, an hour late, the starting gun was fired and the race began.

I was optimistic though. I had trained hard and was ready to run the fastest race of my undistinguished career as an amateur runner. But when I heard my first split (the time announced at the first mile), I was running the slowest race I had ever run. So I picked up the pace. The second split had me running even slower than the first. Despair crept into my thoughts, but I pushed it back and tried to lengthen my stride. The third and fourth splits were even more discouraging, and when I saw the finish line in the distance after the sixth split, I could feel stomach acid sizzling in my throat. If there had been anything in my stomach, I would have lost it on the trail.

WAS IT WORTH IT?

I noticed two things as I approached the finish line. One was my skinny friend Ralph standing there, waiting for me with a big grin on his face. He was a fine track athlete and had left me behind in the middle of the race. The second thing I noticed explained why he was grinning. The air was filled with the sounds of men cussing. These weren't mild expletives. They were the raw and enraged curses of men decrying the fools who had measured the distance of the race. Instead of the standard 6.2 miles of a 10K event, the organizers had mistakenly made it 8.5 miles! I never found out how or why this thing happened, or how the distances between the splits were determined. All I knew was that I was dehydrated and exhausted, and a little relieved that there was an explanation for my unaccountably slow time.

On the way home, Ralph and I stopped for lunch and something to drink. We immediately ordered a pitcher of our favorite cold, carbonated beverage. Ralph poured a glass for each of us and sat down. We raised our glasses, closed our eyes, and took two or three long swallows, letting the cold, refreshing goodness cut through the parched goop lining our throats and stomachs. Ecstasy. We set our glasses down and looked at each other, smiling.

Still savoring the sensation of the drink, Ralph said, "Well, Ben, was it worth it?"

I nodded and answered, "Oh yes!"

It was totally worth it. And had I known how good it would feel to drink that drink at the end of the race, I would have run the middle and end of the race with a far different attitude. It still would have been hard, but there would have been a joy in it. The hurt would have been a good hurt; the hard would have been a good hard. Its rigor would have been an emblem, a symbol and sign of the *agon*, of the good fight.

Why did Jesus go to the Cross to die a brutal and humiliating death? There are a lot of short answers to that question, all confessed by believers for centuries, and all true. He died to make atonement for our sins—that's true. He died because he loved us so very much—truly. He died to glorify his Father—that's true too. He died to put death to death—true, true, true. In one way or another, each of these answers say Jesus suffered and died because *it was worth it*. The cost was great, but what he accomplished was greater.

That is the kind of answer the author of the book of Hebrews gives to the question—but in a startling way. The reason Jesus died, he writes, was for the sake of joy! "Let us . . . [fix] our eyes on Jesus, the pioneer and perfecter of faith. For the joy set before him he endured the cross, scorning its shame" (Hebrews 12:1-2, NIV).

ALL BECAUSE OF HOPE

What would Jesus have said if he had been asked as he was tortured and crucified, "Is it worth it?" If he were able to speak at all, he would have rasped through clenched teeth, "Oh yes." If asked why it was worth it, he would have said, "Because of the joy on the other side of all this." The hope of future joy put the present pain in its place, reducing it to an object of scorn and contempt.

Paul used another metaphor but said the same thing about the weight of his own sufferings: "Therefore we do not lose heart. Though outwardly we are wasting away, yet inwardly we are being renewed day by day. For our light and momentary troubles are achieving for us an eternal glory that far outweighs them all" (2 Corinthians 4:16-17, NIV).

By any normal measure, Paul's personal sufferings could

hardly be considered "light and momentary."[1] But when placed on the scales of eternity and compared to the weight of the glory to come, they were as light as a feather. The hurt was a good hurt, the hard was a good hard, all because of hope.

There are so many ways one can get sidetracked and lose hope in the race. Sometimes it's just because the struggle takes so long—a lifetime, and a lifetime is so daily and mundane. Jesus said the *all*, the *everything* of the *agon*, cannot be paid once for all in one heroic effort. How much easier that would be! To just screw up your courage and in one massive exertion, dump your whole life into Jesus' lap! But it doesn't work that way. No athlete gets to the victory stand in a day. A life lived with Christ must be lived over a lifetime. It is a focused discipline pressed into daily, "a long obedience in the same direction"[2] to life's end. "Then he said to the crowd, 'If any of you wants to be my follower, you must turn from your selfish ways, take up your cross *daily*, and follow me'" (Luke 9:23, italics mine).

THE MYOPIA OF THE MOMENT

It is hope that sustains athletes and Christians. The journey and the race can be desperately hard. But there is joy in the journey because there is joy at the end of the journey. Even better, Jesus not only stands at the finish line, he runs the race with us! The one you run toward is also the one you run with! Through his Spirit, he runs the race and fights the fight with us. As theologian Rubem Alves put it so well, "Hope is hearing the melody of the future. Faith is to dance to it."[3]

Hope can therefore shrivel and die in the myopia of the moment, the spiritual nearsightedness that comes from getting so caught up in a depressing present that you can't see a hopeful future. That is why the word *nevertheless* is such a great gospel word: God looks at our sin and says, "Nevertheless!" It's a great

There is joy in the journey because there is joy at the end of the journey.

hope word too. We can look at wretched circumstances in the moment, from God's eternal perspective, and pronounce over them the great gospel, "Nevertheless!" because the gospel declares that, *nevertheless*, everything that really matters in life has been taken care of:

> *Nothing can ever separate us from God's love. Neither death nor life, neither angels nor demons, neither our fears for today nor our worries about tomorrow—not even the powers of hell can separate us from God's love. No power in the sky above or in the earth below— indeed, nothing in all creation will ever be able to separate us from the love of God that is revealed in Christ Jesus our Lord. (Romans 8:38-39)*

So everything else is just details—fleeting, ephemeral details. The cancer is detail. The depression is detail. The divorce is detail. The lousy job is detail. These things may be disagreeable, annoying, and even abominable in the short term. But as detestable as they may be, they are *nevertheless* not the final word. They will pass away, but our hope, our eternal destiny, is unshakable.

FUNDAMENTALLY SOUND

Perspective is everything. On the fiftieth anniversary of the Allied invasion of Normandy, the great World War II battle to wrest continental Europe from the grip of Hitler, all the major television networks ran programs that included interviews with veterans of the battle. As one would expect, all the interviewees were now quite old.

One of the programs compared the contrasting perspectives of those who fought at Normandy. One aging veteran told of landing on the beach amid unimaginable bloody carnage. He said he looked around at all the death and despaired. He thought, *We're going to lose!* The next interview was with another aging veteran, a US Army reconnaissance officer who told of flying over the entire battle area. He could see the bloodbath on the beach, but he could also see the effectiveness of the marines, the paratroopers' penetration behind enemy lines, and the power of the aerial bombardment. He surveyed the entire scene and thought, *We're going to win!*[4] There was a lot

> **No matter how detestable our present circumstances are, they are not the final word. They will pass away, but our hope, our eternal destiny, is unshakable.**

of suffering and loss, but overall, things were fundamentally sound.

When circumstances aren't as agreeable as I want them to be, I practice a little spiritual discipline that has managed to feed my hope and keep me in joy, nevertheless. I have a long version and a short version: Someone will ask me how I am, and I'll answer, "Other than the fact that all my sins are forgiven and that I'm going to live in heaven eternally in the joy of God, I'm not doing too well." The look on the questioner's face always amuses me. That, and the little irony of saying I'm not doing too well in the face of such magnificent prospects, usually lifts the cloud a bit. That's the long version. The short version is simply to answer, "I'm fundamentally sound." I may be superficially bummed out, sad, frustrated, angry—*whatever!*—but that's the worst I can say about it; it is surface only.

"JUDGE NOT THE LORD BY FEEBLE SENSE"

A more exacting test case is depression. William Cowper (1731–1800), the great Christian poet and mystic, suffered for most of his life from what we might today call bipolar disorder or manic depression. He made several attempts at suicide at age thirty-two. First he tried poisoning, but it failed. He then decided to throw himself into the Thames River; so he hired a horse-drawn cabby to drive him there. But it was one of the foggiest nights of the year, and the cabby drove for more than an hour and couldn't find the bridge and the river. In disgust, Cowper got out of the cab to walk to the bridge. After much wandering, he discovered that he had walked in a circle and had ended up right back at his own doorstep! The next morning he fell upon his knife, but the handle broke. Then he tried hanging himself but was cut down, unconscious but alive.

Some days later he was reading the Bible and came finally to faith in Christ. But he struggled with depression until his death. The last hymn he wrote before descending into a depression that lasted the final seven years of his life begins, "God moves in a mysterious way." He titled it "Light Shining out of Darkness." The faith it expressed was that everything was fundamentally okay, even if the moment did not seem so—even if the "moment" lasted seven years. All that God does and allows he does well and with infinitely wise love.

> *God moves in a mysterious way*
> *His wonders to perform;*
> *He plants his footsteps in the sea,*
> *And rides upon the storm.*
>
> *Deep in unfathomable mines*
> *Of never-failing skill,*
> *He treasures up his bright designs,*
> *And works his sovereign will.*
>
> *Ye fearful saints, fresh courage take,*
> *The clouds ye so much dread,*

Are big with mercy, and shall break
*   In blessings on your head.*

Judge not the Lord by feeble sense,
*   But trust him for his grace:*
Behind a frowning providence
*   He hides a smiling face.*

His purposes will ripen fast
*   Unfolding every hour;*
The bud may have a bitter taste
*   But sweet will be the flower.*

Blind unbelief is sure to err,
*   And scan his work in vain;*
God is his own interpreter
*   And he will make it plain.*[5]

His dear friend, John Newton, with amazing intuition, somehow understood what we do now—that much depression can be a physical disorder. He preached at Cowper's funeral: "He was one of those who came out of great tribulations. He suffered much here . . . but eternity is long enough to make amends for all. For what is all he endured in this life, when compared with the rest which remaineth for the children of God."[6]

"The rest which remaineth for the children of God"— what will that hope be like? My mind goes back to the near ecstacy I felt while guzzling the soft drink with my friend after the exhausting race in Pico Rivera. I am convinced, with C. S. Lewis, that all earthly joys are signposts and little sacraments of the eternal pleasures of God, what he called "the faint, far-off results of those energies which God's creative rapture implanted in matter when He made the worlds." He wondered, what will it be to one day "taste at the fountainhead that stream of which even these lower reaches prove so intoxicating?" Lewis believed that is indeed the Christian hope and that one day "the whole man is to drink joy from the fountain of joy."[7] I think he got the idea from the Bible: "For the Lamb in the midst of the throne will be their shepherd, and he will guide them to springs of living water" (Revelation 7:17, ESV).

For this reason, worship may be the most practical of the means of grace, the disciplines that nourish faith, hope, and love. In worship we are allowed glimpses into eternity, the real world that will never pass away. Those glimpses put the struggles of this present world in their proper place: though they press in on us and wear us down, they won't last. They are producing "for us a glory that vastly outweighs them and will last forever!" For that reason, "we don't look at the troubles we can see now; rather, we fix our gaze on things that cannot be seen. For the things we see now will soon be gone, but the things we cannot see will last forever" (2 Corinthians 4:17-18).

Worship helps us believe and experience that hope. On the Sundays when the worship service was especially rich and glorious, the people in my congregations would often leave church saying, "It's too bad we have to go back into the real world." On those days it was my pleasure to remind them that what they saw and heard in worship was the real world. The trick is to remember the melody of the future and the glories of the life to come during the rest of the week.

CHAPTER 15

SABBATH

MUSCULAR REST

Keep the Sabbath day holy. Don't pursue your own interests on that day, but enjoy the Sabbath and speak of it with delight as the LORD's holy day. Honor the Sabbath in everything you do on that day, and don't follow your own desires or talk idly. Then the LORD will be your delight.
ISAIAH 58:13-14

We cannot destroy Christianity until we first destroy the Christian Sabbath.
VOLTAIRE

FAITH WITHOUT WORKS is dead, but works without faith is deadly. The vigorous life Jesus calls us to is undergirded by what seems to be its opposite: rest. In fact, if the pursuit of holiness and life in the Kingdom is to be robust and vigorous, so must our rest. I learned this, as I have learned most important things, the hard way.

It started with the stabs of pain that would shoot down the backs of my legs. Since I was doing a lot of running at the time while preparing for my third marathon, I thought it must be some kind of muscular stress, so I did a lot more stretching before and after my workouts. But the pain got worse. Sometimes it would awake me in the middle of the night. No matter what position I assumed in the bed, it wouldn't go away. I practically wept with frustration and discomfort.

Finally I did what I should have done much earlier; I went to the doctor. He asked a few questions, manipulated my legs, and sent me to get an X-ray to confirm his diagnosis. The X-ray did: I had two herniated discs in my lower back, as he had suspected. He thought I might be able to avoid surgery if I committed myself to what would probably be about six weeks of complete bed rest. The rest turned out to be on the floor, not on the bed, since my bed was too soft.

I HAD CEASED

I was shaken and perplexed. My body had performed so well for so many years. Now it didn't. What did that mean for my future as a husband and father, as a man? And there was the church I had started three years before: I was pretty much all the pastoral staff the church had. Who would do the preaching? Who would lead the elders and plan the worship services? *There is one positive in the six weeks of rest*, I thought: *at least I can get a lot of reading done.* But that didn't happen, since the pain medication and muscle relaxant I was taking made me drowsy and my eyes wouldn't focus well. I read exactly one book in six weeks.

Mostly what I did at the beginning of those six weeks was hurt and worry and cry. The smallest thing would happen to me—a cross word, a morbid thought, even a telephone call from a well-wishing friend—and I would find tears running down my face uncontrollably. Walking was so painful that every trip to the restroom was a race between my tolerance of the pain and my need to relieve myself. The pain sometimes won, and I'd have to lie down on the restroom floor for a while to gain the strength to use the toilet. It was all so humiliating and emasculating. The worst was watching my sweet wife do all the work of the household. We had two small children at the time—actually three, counting me— and she bore the brunt of so much. I couldn't do anything that mattered, it seemed: as an athlete, as a father and husband, as a pastor, as a provider, as a man. I had been shut down, stopped and stymied; I had ceased.

Then one day during the third or fourth week of my ordeal, the thought dawned: The one thing I could do was pray. It didn't seem like a lot to me, but at least it was something. So I asked my wife, Lauretta, to get me a copy of the church directory. I purposed to pray through the entire membership of the church every day, person by person, presenting before God the name of each and every man, woman, boy, and girl. It usually took about two hours. Don't misunderstand; it wasn't piety or a deep belief in the power of prayer that motivated me. If it had, I would have prayed a lot more when I was well. What was driving me to pray was boredom and impotence. But soon the times of prayer became sweeter than any I had ever known. A new sense of intimacy with God and my people was emerging. The two hours flew by.

"STUPID"

I thought, *Wouldn't it be nice if I could keep this up when I was back on my feet and back to work?* One day near the end of my convalescence, I was thinking that thought, and I said to God, *Father, I've enjoyed these times of prayer so much. It's too bad I won't have as much time to pray when I get back to work.* His response was swift and blunt; he said, *Stupid.* It was in a nice tone of voice, but that's what he said. *You have the same twenty-four hours when you are well as when you are sick,* he continued. *The trouble with you, Ben, is that when you are well you think you're in control; and when you are sick you know you aren't.* Those words changed my life. Prayer—and the significance of words like *cease* and *stop*—has never been the same since. My understanding of what it means to fight the good fight was also transformed.

"To cease or stop" is roughly the meaning of the Hebrew word translated *Sabbath* in the Bible. To cease or stop working one day out of seven is a command, one of the ten big ones, right there with the commands to have no other gods, worship no idols, and not to murder or commit adultery. But like the rest, it is more than a command; it was given as a gift, a permission, really. Jesus went out of his way to say that this command in particular was designed especially with humans in mind. "The Sabbath was made to meet the needs of people, and not people to meet the requirements of the Sabbath" (Mark 2:27). As with all of God's commands, the command to keep the Sabbath holy is both for God's glory and our own good. There is no conflict between the two whatsoever; whatever magnifies the Lover of our souls enriches our souls. What God commands, he blesses; the commands themselves are blessings. Those with eyes to see can exclaim, "How I delight in your commands! How I love them!" (Psalm 119:47).

Like the other commandments, the Sabbath is more than a command; it was given as a gift, a permission, really.

What are the blessings of the Sabbath for those who would fight the good fight? The first is obvious: the *agon* can be exhausting; fighting the good fight can grind us down; running the race can be discouraging. When God commanded the Sabbath, he spoke a profound word of grace to those who strive—he said we not only *must* rest, but we *may* rest, joyfully.

In the Bible the Sabbath command is linked to God's work in the six days of creation and his rest on the seventh day.[1] We should keep the Sabbath because God did. At the end of each day as he finished his work, the Scripture says he punctuated it with this happy judgment: "And God saw that it was good." It was exactly what he had in mind. It was complete. But on the sixth day when he crowned all his good work by making a man and a woman, "God looked over all he had made, and he saw that it was *very* good." The creation was now more than the sum of its parts; "good" times six equals "very good." Then on the next day, the seventh, he rested.

But why? Was it because he was tired and needed a nap? Not God; he doesn't slumber or sleep. As good as a nap can be, God's rest was of a different, sweeter kind: it was the kind of rest one enjoys when everything is finished and whole and very good; when there is nothing left to do but to savor and celebrate it, to rejoice and be glad. That is exactly what God did on the seventh day, and what he commands us to do too, and for the same reason. Since "the LORD takes pleasure in all he has made" (Psalm 104:31), we should too. We, too, should stop each week and rest as God rested, not because our work is done, but because God's is, and in him ours will one day be complete. In God we may rest in the assurance that all is finished and guaranteed and that, as Julian of Norwich famously put it, "All shall be well and all shall be well, and all manner of things shall be well."[2]

A RHYTHM AND A PATTERN

God built a rhythm of work and joyful rest into creation, into the very structure of the world. Break the rhythm and the melody goes bad. It's as though our bodies, be they Christian bodies or not, were programmed for this rhythm. In the aftermath of the French Revolution, the Sabbath was abolished and replaced by one day of rest in ten. Voltaire reportedly said, "We cannot destroy Christianity until we first destroy the Christian Sabbath." But the experiment was a disaster: men and women crumbled under the strain and animals literally collapsed in the streets.

There is also a pattern to this rhythm: it moves not from work to rest, but from rest to work. The biblical reckoning of the day is not from sunup to sundown, as we reckon it, but from sundown to sunup. The days in the Genesis account of creation are measured, not from morning to evening, but from evening to morning: "And evening passed and morning came, marking the first day," ". . . the second day," and so on (Genesis 1:5, 8, 13, 19, 23, 31), with each new day beginning not with people getting up to work, but with people lying down to rest! Think of it: What's the first thing we do each day—get up to work or lie down to sleep? We begin each day with rest, and as we rest, who runs the world, who does the work? God does. Each morning we wake up into his great work to do ours—or better, to find our place in his. Fighting the good fight is not starting the fight but joining it, entering into the *agon*. From beginning to end, from sunup to sundown, it is God who works and fights and runs, and we who follow.

The order or pattern of creation is the same as the order or pattern of salvation: In all things we move not from work to grace, but from grace to work—otherwise grace is not grace, but wages! The message of the Sabbath, and of each day of the week, is grace. It sets us straight on what Peter Kreeft calls the "grammar of existence"—that God is God and we are not. We can let him run the universe; all we need do is find our place in his scheme. Fighting the good fight can press us down and bury us under its weight if we forget this. But the Sabbath speaks grace into the lives of driven, harassed servants of Christ. It says to us all, "You may stop now—no, you must stop now—at least for a day."

A DECLARATION OF WAR

But the Sabbath is much more than rest from or for the fight. Otherwise the Sabbath is defined by the fight. No, to keep the Sabbath actually is to fight. The Sabbath is an act of defiance, a declaration of war against a world system that tells us that all that we are is what we do, and that unless we *do*, we won't *be*. A grim sign hung over the entrance to one of the Nazi death camps: *Arbeit Macht Frei*, which means "work makes you free." Jews destined for the ovens were greeted by the lie that they would survive only if they worked hard. The world tells the same lie. Too many zealous believers have baptized the lie and lived as though everything depends on their efforts. To rest is to fight against the world's lie.

> The order or pattern of creation is the same as the order or pattern of salvation: In all things we move not from work to grace, but from grace to work—otherwise grace is not grace, but wages!

The Sabbath speaks freedom to these earnest slaves. Deuteronomy gives another theological rationale for the day that is slightly different from the one found in Exodus 20. It mandates the Sabbath and gives this explanation: "Remember that you were once slaves in Egypt, but the LORD your God brought you out with his strong hand and powerful arm. That is why the LORD your God has commanded you to rest on the Sabbath day" (Deuteronomy 5:15). God is saying, "Once you were slaves and had to work or die, but now you are free—don't ever forget it. Be sure to observe the Sabbath so you don't. Stop working once a week to remember that you are free, not slaves."

ON WINGS LIKE EAGLES

The Sabbath is therefore a freedom day; keeping it is an act of defiance and rebellion in a world that lives under the slavery of work. It is a weekly rebuttal of the worldly dogma that we justify our existence and sustain ourselves by achievement. The world may say, "If you think nobody cares if you're alive, try missing a few car payments," or "If you haven't got an ulcer, you're not carrying your share of the load." The Sabbath says the opposite. The command to keep the Sabbath holy empowers us to deflate all the imperial claims that work, even so-called Christian work, would make on our lives. It enables us to look work in the eye and say, "No! I am not your slave! I'm stopping for the next twenty-four hours. In Christ I am free. My future well-being is in his hands, not in how well my hands serve you." Joy! To rest is to be a subversive.

Therefore, the beauty of the command to keep the Sabbath is that it is a command. We would rarely rest if we were given the choice. We are like children who desperately need to take a nap but won't unless they're ordered to. We need to be ordered by the Almighty to rest, or else we'll keep on obeying the orders of almighty work. There can be a great delight in looking at a pile of work and saying on the Sabbath, "No, not today; my Master says you'll just have to wait until tomorrow."

Keeping the Sabbath is a weekly rebuttal of the worldly dogma that we justify our existence and sustain ourselves by achievement.

The common wisdom of the world, and the default mode of worldly Christian faith, is "Don't just stand there—do something." When in doubt, get busy and work harder. It's so easy to mistake that for the voice of God. But in the Sabbath, God commands us: "Don't just do something—stand there."

To do this is to be empowered the way an eagle is empowered for flight as it perches atop a high crag. "But those who trust in the LORD will find new strength. They will soar high on wings like eagles. They will run and not grow weary. They will walk and not faint" (Isaiah 40:31). As big and as majestic in flight as eagles are, their wings, or the pectoral and back muscles that flap their wings, are actually weak in proportion to the size of their wings. Their physiques are nothing like those of the muscular little hummingbirds that flap their wings at the speed of an airplane propeller. Instead, an eagle must rely on the sensors God has put inside his nostrils. As the bird perches atop a high crag, the eagle's sensors quietly take in the velocity and warmth of the thermals, the winds that rise up from the depths of the canyon below. When the thermals are just right, the eagle folds its wings to its sides and casts itself into the depths, plummeting to the rocks below, falling faster and faster until its sensors register the right moment to spread its wings. Then the eagle shoots back up into the sky and soars! It isn't the exertion of frantic labor that sends it flying so gracefully, but quiet confidence in the wind. There are times when the eagle does flap its wings, but the critical moments are when it doesn't.

It is the same for those who fight the good fight and run the race. *Wind*, as you may know, is one of the words for the Spirit in the Bible. And when we allow him to carry us during our periods of rest, we, too, may find ourselves soaring.

CHAPTER 16

MORTIFICATION OF SIN
WITH EXTREME PREJUDICE

So put to death the sinful, earthly things lurking within you.
COLOSSIANS 3:5

Be killing sin, or it will be killing you.
JOHN OWEN

THE FIRST TIME evil appears in the Bible (see Genesis 3:1-5), it sounds sympathetic and friendly:

- Smilingly, the serpent engages Eve in a theological conversation about the nuances of God's will ("Did God really say . . . ?");
- then he urges her to consider an alternative interpretation of God's warning ("You won't die!");
- then he suggests that she examine more closely his real motives in giving it ("God knows that your eyes will be opened . . . ");
- finally he invites her to strike out on a bold and fulfilling course in life ("You will be like God, knowing both good and evil").

The next time evil appears, it is exposed for the fraud that it is. As Cain plots to murder his brother, Abel, God warns him that sin plots violence too, against Cain, lurking at his door like the savage predator Cain is about to become. "Sin," he says, "is crouching at the door. Its desire is for you, but you must rule over it" (Genesis 4:7, ESV). If he doesn't master the beast, the beast will master him. The rest, as we know, is history. The theme runs throughout the Bible to its very end, where evil is variously portrayed as a ravenous lion; a dragon; a seven-headed beast; and a foul, leering whore, drunk on the blood of God's people. The warning is everywhere, implicit and explicit: "Stay alert! Watch out for your great enemy, the devil. He prowls around like a roaring lion, looking for someone to devour" (1 Peter 5:8).

VOMIT FROM THE HEART

Sin is a predator, its prey is us, and the only reasonable response is to kill the beast that would kill us—to, as John Owen put it, "be killing sin, or it will be killing you." But there is a complication: evil is not just "out there" in the world; it's inside us too, as close as can be, in our very hearts. Using a different metaphor, Jesus said:

> *It's what comes out of a person that pollutes: obscenities, lusts, thefts, murders, adulteries, greed, depravity, deceptive dealings, carousing, mean looks, slander, arrogance, foolishness—all these are vomit from the heart. There is the source of your pollution.* (Mark 7:20-23, *The Message*)

What can one do when the resident evil is intimately resident, as inside as it can possibly be, in the heart? The principle still applies: you kill it. The biblical directive is uncompromising: "Put to death the sinful, earthly things *lurking* within you," things like, "sexual immorality, impurity, lust, and evil desires" (Colossians 3:5, italics mine).

God is a warrior. When we believed the gospel, we took sides in a cosmic, spiritual con-

Sin is a predator, its prey is us, and the only reasonable response is to kill the beast that would kill us.

flict that is infinitely more lethal than any conflict fought on earth. Remember John White's words: "Wars on earth are but tremors felt from an earthquake light-years away. The Christian's war takes place at the epicenter of the earthquake."[1] And where is the epicenter? It's in the scariest place imaginable—the heart. The war is not fought on foreign soil; it's fought at home. "We have met the enemy and he is us,"[2] a truth that made the apostle Paul groan:

I know that nothing good lives in me, that is, in my sinful nature. I want to do what is right, but I can't. I want to do what is good, but I don't. I don't want to do what is wrong, but I do it anyway. But if I do what I don't want to do, I am not really the one doing wrong; it is sin living in me that does it. I have discovered this principle of life—that when I want to do what is right, I inevitably do what is wrong. I love God's law with all my heart. But there is another power within me that is at war with my mind. This power makes me a slave to the sin that is still within me. Oh, what a miserable person I am! Who will free me from this life that is dominated by sin and death? (Romans 7:18-24)

FREED FROM THE CONSEQUENCES, BUT NOT THE STRUGGLE

This would be very, very bad news indeed were it not for the very, very good news of the gospel that immediately followed Paul's lament: "So now there is no condemnation for those who belong to Christ Jesus. And because you belong to him,

The epicenter of the Christian's war against sin is in the scariest place imaginable—the heart.

the power of the life-giving Spirit has freed you from the power of sin that leads to death" (Romans 8:1-2).

Freed from the power and consequences of sin that lead to death, those who belong to Christ Jesus live in the vibrant hope and confidence that nothing can ever separate them from the love of God, absolutely nothing; death can't and life can't; angels can't and demons can't; not even the powers of hell have any power whatsoever to undo what God has done for us in Christ. So Paul, and everyone who believes the gospel Paul preached, can declare with a gigantic, joyful sigh of relief, "If God is for us, who can ever be against us?" (Romans 8:31). The battle has been won, and the war is over. "We have escaped like a bird from a hunter's trap" (Psalm 124:7).

All of that is true but with this crucial caveat: though we have been freed from the *consequences* of sin—eternal judgment and hell—we are not yet released from the *struggle* against sin. Our redemption is as decisively sure and complete as Christ's resurrection from the dead. We have, in fact, died to the sin that Christ bore on the Cross and have been raised with him to new life. That miracle accomplished, we may now fight against the sin that once held us in its deathly grip, no longer as sin's slaves but as God's children. "Since you have been raised to new life with Christ," we are told, "set your sights on the realities of heaven," and "put to death the sinful, earthly things lurking within you" (Colossians 3:1, 5). We are no longer sinners struggling to be the children of God, but children of God who struggle against sin, in the power of the Holy Spirit. We put sin to death, not so we may live, but because we do live.

THE ALREADY AND THE NOT YET

New Testament theologian Oscar Cullmann coined a metaphor for this new gospel reality: he called it "the already and the not yet." The "already" could be compared to the major event on June 6, 1944—D-Day in World War II—when the Allies successfully established a beachhead on the Normandy coast and in so doing effectively defeated the Nazis. But though the decisive battle had been won, there was still a lot of fighting ahead, a lot of "not yet," including the bloody Battle of the Bulge, before the German government surrendered unconditionally, on May 8, 1945—nearly a year later. A lot had to happen before D-Day was consummated on VE Day, Victory in Europe Day.

For the Christian, there is really only one more big thing to happen in history: Christ has already come, Christ has already died, Christ has already been raised, and Christ is already seated at the right hand of the Father in heaven. The last big thing, the "not yet," will be the return of Christ to consummate his victory. We've been living in the last days since Christ ascended into heaven.

So until Christ returns, there is a war to fight. Our enemies are what they have always been, what classic Christian thought has called the devil, the world, and the flesh, or our old sinful nature. No attempt to understand the Christian's struggle would be complete without taking them into account, beginning with the work of the devil, the enemy of our souls, the Accuser, the Confuser (*diabolos*), the Liar, and the Murderer, whose work Jesus came to destroy.[3]

We also struggle against what the Bible calls the world: the systems and values and idols of our culture that set themselves up against the knowledge of God. The world is a powerful and subtle enemy, because it is ruled by a powerful and subtle devil. Archbishop William Temple said the world is like a jewelry store that has been broken into by vandals, who have not stolen anything, but simply switched the price tags so that cheap and tawdry things are priced highly, and precious things priced cheaply or discarded as worthless. The devil and the world have been exposed and defeated at the

Cross, and they will end up in the trash heap of eternity. Even so, they still have their allure and can take with them to the trash heap all who give themselves over to their ways. So John wrote:

> *Don't love the world's ways. Don't love the world's goods. Love of the world squeezes out love for the Father. Practically everything that goes on in the world—wanting your own way, wanting everything for yourself, wanting to appear important—has nothing to do with the Father. It just isolates you from him. The world and all its wanting, wanting, wanting is on the way out—but whoever does what God wants is set for eternity.* (1 John 2:15-17, *The Message*)

PIANO STRINGS AND GARBAGE

Truly the world is the devil's realm, and no one can love the world and at the same time love the Father. But our struggle is not ultimately against the devil, as dangerous as he is, or the world. The heart of our struggle is our heart. The devil and his world would never get a hearing from us if there wasn't something in us that wanted to listen. Our heart is like a piano: Open the top and you will see a lot of piano wires, each string corresponding to a note on the piano keyboard. You can sing a note into the mass of piano strings and watch as the string that matches the note sung vibrates and resonates with your voice. The world and the devil are always singing to us, and when we hear a melody we like, we start vibrating and dancing to it.

Professor Charles Kraft uses a different analogy: He says the devil and his demons are like rats. Rats are attracted to garbage, and as long as garbage is available to the rats, no amount of rat traps will keep them away—in a sense, the rats aren't the problem; the garbage is. Get rid of the garbage and the rats will be less of a problem. The devil and the world feed on the garbage we keep in our heart, and then they also sell more garbage to us—what a deal![4]

> The heart of our struggle is our heart. The devil and his world would never get a hearing from us if there wasn't something in us that wanted to listen.

Piano strings and garbage: two analogies of sin in the heart. I think another picture, that of a resident traitor, is even better. The seventeenth-century theologian John Owen wrote, "However strong a castle may be, if a treacherous party resides inside (ready to betray at the first opportunity possible), the castle cannot be kept safe from the enemy. Traitors occupy our own hearts, ready to side with every temptation and to surrender to them all."[5]

EXTREME PREJUDICE

This warning takes us back to Paul's command to "put to death the sinful, earthly things lurking within you" (Colossians 3:5). Have you ever thought of your sin in this way—as an alien enemy disguised as a friend, a spy, a mole, waiting and watching within, looking for a chance to bring your life down?

C. S. Lewis linked his conversion to Christianity with this startling insight. When he looked into his soul, he said, "I found what appalled me; a zoo of lusts, a bedlam of ambitions, a nursery of fears, a harem of fondled hatreds. My name was legion."[6] If traitors are executed in war, how much more should they be killed in this most lethal of combats, the battle for our souls?

A term sometimes used in law enforcement applies here: If a criminal is armed and on the verge of opening fire on a helpless victim or a police officer, the police will react with "extreme prejudice," which means they will shoot, not to wound, but to kill. The traitors within are not harmless little peccadilloes, innocuous moral handicaps; they are deeply and savagely malevolent; they are out to destroy us and should be treated with extreme prejudice. They are the old you, the old man or woman who was crucified with Christ but who lingers in your soul like a zombie, the "living dead," seeking still to consume you. The seventeenth-century poet George Herbert spoke of his fight with sin as fighting against the man he once was and vowed to Christ:

> Yet by confession will I come
> Into Thy conquest. Though I can do nought
> Against Thee, in Thee I will overcome
>   The man who once against Thee fought.[7]

THE INVISIBLE WAR

What we see out in the world is the tumultuous drama of rulers and nations conspiring against the Lord and each other, "seething, struggling, laboring, dying."[8] But the real fight is within our soul, where an eternal conflict is ever raging. On the outcome of this internal fight rests, ultimately, the outcome of the outer struggle of history. Andrée Seu writes:

> You will never see someone "fight the good fight of the faith" [because] it all happened when you weren't there, alone on a long country walk, just between him and the Lord. That's where the blood and sweat and the dying occurred. By the time you spotted the fellow out in public—in the visible battlefield, or at a PTO meeting, or pushing away some lucrative job offer, or not leaving his wife—the heavy lifting was already done. One often detects a certain peace in the presence of such people.[9]

The fight is daily, moment-by-moment, a continuous brawl, fought with extreme prejudice. We would find this struggle hopeless and exhausting were it not for the power of God to sustain us and the hope of his promise to bless those who stand and fight, believing that "God blesses those who patiently endure testing and temptation. Afterward they will receive the crown of life that God has promised to those who love him" (James 1:12).

CHAPTER 17

LEARNING TO LOVE THE GOOD

WOW!

And we all, who with unveiled faces contemplate the Lord's glory, are being transformed into his image with ever-increasing glory, which comes from the Lord, who is the Spirit.
2 CORINTHIANS 3:18, NIV

Grant me, O Lord, to know what I ought to know, to love what I ought to love, to praise what delights thee most, to value what is precious in thy sight, to hate what is offensive to thee.
THOMAS Á KEMPIS

MY FAVORITE PICTURE of what happens when one is converted is G. K. Chesterton's. He said the unconverted are like people born upside down, head stuck in the sand, feet dangling in the sky. From that posture, heaven and eternity and the things of God seem light and insubstantial, of no consequence; the earth, which truly is light and insubstantial and passing away, is what seems solid and real.

To be set right side up—to be converted—is to see things as they really are, head in the heavens where it belongs, feet firmly on the ground where they belong. The converted can walk the earth and not stumble because they now see where to walk. Have you heard the saying "too heavenly minded to be any earthly good"? That's wrong. The truth is quite the opposite; for the only way to be any earthly good, with your feet walking the earth, is to be heavenly minded, with your head in heaven.

Chesterton's picture is a metaphor for the vibrant reality the apostle Paul describes:

> *Since you have been raised to new life with Christ, set your sights on the realities of heaven, where Christ sits in the place of honor at God's right hand. Think about the things of heaven, not the things of earth. For you died to this life, and your real life is hidden with Christ in God. And when Christ, who is your life, is revealed to the whole world, you will share in all his glory.* (Colossians 3:1-4)

GOOD VIOLENCE

To believe in Christ is to be so profoundly unified with Christ's life as to share in his resurrection from the dead. But, of course, Christ would not have been raised from the dead if he had not first died! So the gospel declares that Christ died for our sins and "was raised to life to make us right with God" (Romans 4:25). Therefore, to be identified with Christ in his resurrection by necessity also means to be identified with him in his death to sin, and to live a life that actively seeks, in the power of the same Spirit that raised Christ, "[to] put to death the sinful, earthly things lurking within you" (Colossians 3:5). This calls for a massive "renovation of the heart"[1]—a lifelong process by which you put on the very character of Christ and actually "share his divine nature" (2 Peter 1:4).

The renovation begins with repentance. Repentance has a negative side and a positive side: on the one hand, it means to die to what you were; and on the other hand, to come alive to what you are to become. The death part is an act of spiritual violence, of "extreme prejudice" toward evil and darkness (see the previous chapter). François Fénelon counseled: "You must violently resist the tides of the world. Violently give up all that holds you back from God. Violently turn your will over to God to do his will alone."

It has taken me a long time to understand the negative, or death side of repentance. At first, I thought of repentance simply as remorse, feeling bad about the sin in my life, or fearing its consequences: the shame, pain, and punishment that might come because of my transgressions. While the terror of punishment for evil is part of it, true repentance is much deeper. True repentance is godly grief that a holy God was wronged when I sinned.

"It is one thing to mourn for sin because it exposes us to hell," wrote eighteenth-century theologian Gardiner Spring, "and another to mourn for it because it is an infinite evil; one thing to mourn for it because it is injurious to ourselves, and another thing to mourn for it because it is wrong and offensive to God. It is one thing to be terrified; another, to be humbled." To be humbled is to do violence against your pride.

FROM ME-CENTERED TO GOD-CENTERED

I also mistakenly thought of repentance as self-improvement, the idea that I had repented because I'd set out to improve myself. True repentance is not self-improvement but self-surrender, another deathly blow to pride. As usual, C. S. Lewis put it so very well:

> Fallen man is not simply an imperfect creature who needs improvement; he is a rebel who must lay down his arms. . . . This process of surrender—this movement full speed astern—is what Christians call repentance. Now repentance is no fun at all. It is something much harder than merely eating humble pie. It means unlearning all the self-conceit and self-will that we have been training ourselves into for thousands of years. It means killing part of yourself, undergoing a kind of death.[2]

Understanding exactly what I was saying no to in repentance has not come easily, because it means being delivered from myself, of rejecting the radical "me-centeredness" of sin—the pride, egotism, and self-will that make sin so evil. It is indeed death to the old self because true repentance is radically God-centered.

But it has taken me even longer to grasp the positive, or resurrection side of repentance, and for the same reason: true repentance is radically God-centered. If the negative, deathly side of repentance is ending my love affair with myself, the positive side is learning to fall in love with God. It was just a short sentence by Frederick Buechner that started me thinking about this. He wrote, "True repentance spends less time looking at the past and saying, 'I'm sorry,' than to the future and saying 'Wow!'"[3]

> If the negative, deathly side of repentance is ending my love affair with myself, the positive side is learning to fall in love with God.

WOW!

Wow! is what Irenaeus had in mind when he said, "The glory of God is man fully alive, and the life of man is the vision of God." The greater glory of God is not to be seen in galaxies and snow-capped mountain peaks but in people, made in God's image, who reflect God's image and glory out into the world. God is never more glorified than when his people gaze adoringly at his beauty and say, "Wow!" For when they do, they themselves become a little more "Wow!" Really! The Bible says so: "And we all, who with unveiled faces contemplate the Lord's glory, are being transformed into his image with ever-increasing glory, which comes from the Lord, who is the Spirit" (2 Corinthians 3:18, NIV).

Wow, indeed. The reason you say "No!" to sin is so you may say "Yes!" to the glorious prospect that you "may one day be a creature which, if you saw it now, you would be strongly tempted to worship."[4] That is the goal of repentance: to so gloriously reflect the glory of God that you are transformed into his glory; to become

God is never more glorified than when his people gaze adoringly at his beauty and say, "Wow!"

like Jesus who "radiates God's own glory and expresses the very character of God" (Hebrews 1:3).

The devil can't understand this. Our Wow! is his Ugh! In C. S. Lewis's *The Screwtape Letters*, the demon Screwtape expresses his disgust for God's regard for humanity to his nephew Wormwood:

> One must face the fact that all the talk about
> His love for men, and His service being perfect
> freedom, is not (as one would gladly believe) mere
> propaganda, but an appalling truth. He really *does*
> want to fill the universe with a lot of loathsome
> little replicas of Himself—creatures whose life, on
> its miniature scale, will be qualitatively like His
> own, not because He has absorbed them but because
> their wills freely conform to His.[5]

Wow! was what moved Moses to such reckless longing that he asked God to let him see what would destroy him: the face of God unfiltered. God graciously refused, explaining that "no one may see me and live" (Exodus 33:20). But when Augustine read this, he prayed what I think must have passed through Moses' mind: "Hast thou said, 'No one may see me and live?' Then let me die."

Wow! was what Dante was thinking when he brought the *Divine Comedy* to an end. Having passed through the circles of Hell and through Purgatory before ascending through the highest heights of heaven, he finally stood gazing into the Godhead. He wanted to describe what he saw, but words left him, and all he could do was describe the effect the vision of God had on him. As he looked at God, he discovered that something wonderful was happening to his desire and will, the very thing that all true repentance longs for: "But now my desire and will were revolved like a wheel which is moved evenly, by the love that moves the sun and other stars."[6]

THE EXPULSIVE POWER OF A NEW AFFECTION

That's what we need when we repent of our sin. The goal of repentance is to have your desires and affections transformed and moved by the same divine love that makes the stars and planets move together in harmony through this vast universe, each in harmony with the will of God.

Wow! can even be experienced as a sweet sadness and temporary self-loathing, as God said it would be for the Babylonian exiles. Essentially he told them, "In spite of what you've been, I'm going to treat you so well that you'll hate yourself for what you've been."[7]

It is not enough to hate evil; we must develop what Thomas Chalmers called "the expulsive power of a new affection." In the Greek myth, when Ulysses sailed past the Isle of the Sirens, he stopped his crew's ears with wax so they couldn't hear the Sirens' song. Then he had them tie him to the mast, so he couldn't respond to it. The Sirens' music was so seductive that no man could resist the urge to jump overboard to swim to where they were. Everyone who ever tried died. Ulysses was a negative goodness. However, in another myth, Orpheus sat on the deck and survived by playing his own music, a music far more beautiful than the Sirens'. His was a positive goodness.

It's not enough to hate what is wrong; you must love what is right—for the truth is, you won't adequately hate what is wrong unless you love what is right. A man in love will spurn all other women, not because he thinks them all worthless, but because his love for his beloved makes them all seem so. Thomas á Kempis prayed for both godly hate and godly love to motivate him. He asked God, "Grant me, O Lord, to know what I ought to know, to love what I ought to love, to praise what delights thee most, to value what is precious in thy sight, to hate what is offensive to thee."

> It's not enough to hate what is wrong; you must love what is right.

Paul advised Timothy both to run from what was bad and to pursue what was good: "But you, Timothy, are a man of God; so *run from* all these evil things. *Pursue* righteousness and a godly life, along with faith, love, perseverance, and gentleness" (1 Timothy 6:11, italics mine).

We need both hate and love, but love is the more critical of the two.

PRACTICING WOW!

How do you grow your love for God's goodness? By gazing at him, by practicing Wow!—in essence by praying what David prayed when he asked God to grant him the "one thing worth being concerned about" (Luke 10:42):

> The one thing I ask of the LORD—
>   the thing I seek most—
> is to live in the house of the LORD all the days of my life,
>   delighting in the LORD's perfections
>   and meditating in his Temple. (Psalm 27:4)

Delighting and *meditating* are big words, covering the whole spectrum of the spiritual disciplines: things like worship and prayer and Scripture and fellowship and service. None of these activities, in and of themselves, can change the desires of your heart; only the Holy Spirit can do that, and Jesus said the Spirit is like the wind[8]—free and wild and uncontrollable. You can no more learn to love God than you can will the wind to blow. Human achievement is worthless, but not faithful human effort. So while you can't control the wind, you can spread your sail, so that when the wind blows, you are moved in the direction it is blowing.

The disciplines work like that; like spreading a sail, they position you to receive what God is only too ready to give: himself and all that he is, what we know as the fruit of the Spirit (to mix a metaphor)—"love, joy, peace, patience,

kindness, goodness, faithfulness, gentleness, and self-control"
(Galatians 5:22-23). In fact, even the desire to position your-
self to receive God's gifts is a sure sign that the wind of his
Spirit is already blowing through your soul.

THE TRAVAIL OF HIS SOUL IN ME

The disciplines are always to be practiced in hope, for growth
in grace and love are part of the *agon* of the Christian life,
very much like the pain of childbirth. Practicing them is often
hard and painful, requiring
great patience and endurance,
and not reaching completion
until the day Christ returns.[9]
Our Wow! is future-oriented,
sometimes like an exhausted
mother's excruciating efforts—
what used to be called her
"travail"—who hangs in and pushes until the baby is birthed.
All that keeps her going is the hope of the child to be born.

Even the desire to position yourself to receive God's gifts is a sure sign that the wind of his Spirit is already blowing through your soul.

I keep the words of hymn writer Dora Greenwell right in
front of me on my desk:

> *And O, that He fulfilled may see*
> *The travail of His soul in me,*
> *And with His work contented be,*
> *As I with my dear Savior.*[10]

I thank God that whatever "travail" I experience, it is also the travail of Christ's soul in me. (Christ's soul is his life—that's the meaning of the Greek word [*psuche*] behind our English word *soul*.) He is really involved! That brings a comfort and a courage that is inexpressible. Whatever I am now, good and bad, is not what I will ultimately be, for my "real life is hidden with Christ in God," and when Christ, who is my life, is revealed to the world, I will be revealed too and "will share in all his glory" (Colossians 3:3-4). When I die, that will not be the last anyone will see of me! To fight the good fight, finish the race, and keep the faith is to know what Luther knew:

> This life, therefore, is not righteousness, but growth in righteousness, not health, but healing, not being but becoming, not rest but exercise. We are not yet what we shall be, but we are growing toward it; the process is not yet finished but it is going on. This is not the end but it is the road; all does not yet gleam in glory but all is being purified.[11]

Wow!

CHAPTER 18

HARDHEADED LOVE
THE LOVE MOST LIKE GOD'S

May the Lᴏʀᴅ punish me severely if I allow anything but death
to separate us!
RUTH 1:17

I'm looking for a hard headed woman.
CAT STEVENS

THREE WIDOWS ARE walking west from Moab to Israel, all
stricken by the same tragedy: Naomi, the oldest of the three,
has lost her husband, Elimelech, and her two sons, Mahlon
and Kilion. Years before, she and Elimelech had emigrated
from Israel to Moab during a severe famine. Her sons had
married women of that nation, and now all the men in her
life have died. Naomi is a stranger alone in a strange land,
and she wants to go home. With her are her sons' widows,
her daughters-in-law, Orpah and Ruth.

One of Naomi's daughters-in-law is a hardheaded woman.
"Hard Headed Woman" was the title of a popular song Cat
Stevens wrote in the 1970s about the kind of woman he
needed in his life. *Hardheaded* was a metaphor for the kind
of stubborn, unfailing, unswerving, and unsentimental love
by which a woman would take him for himself just as he was

but love him too much to let him stay that way. She would never leave him, or leave him alone; her love would make him the best man he could be, and if he found her, he said, "I know the rest of my life will be blessed."[1]

In our story, Ruth is the hardheaded woman, and she's also a Moabite, a woman of Moab. I call attention to this to underline the sheer improbability of such a woman having a place in the Bible, much less a whole book devoted to her. The Jews hated the Moabites, and the Moabites hated the Jews. Even the name spoke of shame: it sounded like the Hebrew "from my father," an allusion to the incest of Lot's daughters. After the destruction of Sodom and Gomorrah, they got their father drunk and had sex with him so they could be assured of having children. Every mention of Moab in the Scriptures is negative, so much so that no Ammonite or Moabite was ever to enter the congregation of God, even to the tenth generation, and every Jew was obliged never to promote the welfare and prosperity of a Moabite.[2]

SOLITARY, POOR, NASTY, BRUTISH, AND SHORT

Adding to the drama of this hardheaded woman is the fact that the backdrop of the story is the book of Judges, a time when the life of most Hebrews could be described as "solitary, poor, nasty, brutish, and short."[3] In fact, in the Bible, the book of Ruth is placed right after the book of Judges. Apostasy and treachery were egregious, and the wars were savage.

Ruth begins just after the appalling account of the gang

rape and murder of a scoundrel's concubine at the end of Judges. That text goes into detail about the dismemberment of her corpse—twelve pieces of her, one for each of the twelve tribes!—and the fratricidal slaughter of the entire tribe of Benjamin for this outrage.

This is the context of a remarkable exchange between Ruth and Naomi. Naomi has just urged her daughters-in-law not to go with her to Israel but to stay among their people in Moab where they can find new husbands. Orpah finally agrees to turn back, but not Ruth:

> But Ruth replied, "Don't ask me to leave you and turn back. Wherever you go, I will go; wherever you live, I will live. Your people will be my people, and your God will be my God. Wherever you die, I will die, and there I will be buried. May the LORD punish me severely if I allow anything but death to separate us!" When Naomi saw that Ruth was determined to go with her, she said nothing more. (Ruth 1:16-18)

"May the LORD punish me severely if I allow anything but death to separate us!" These are the words of a hardheaded woman; that's the kind of thing hardheaded people say about their promises.

A FORTY-TWO-YEAR-OLD PROMISE

Have you heard of Robertson McQuilkin and Samwise Gamgee? Robertson McQuilkin is a hardheaded man. A gifted speaker and leader, McQuilkin had been president of Columbia Bible College, now Columbia International University, when in March 1990 he resigned his post in order to care full-time for his wife, Muriel, whose Alzheimer's disease had been steadily robbing her of mental health.

Friends and supporters begged McQuilkin to stay on; they would help with Muriel's care, even donate money to help pay for her care in an institution. The problem with all this was that the only time she was happy was when her husband was near her. When he left the house, she would be terrified that she had lost him and would anxiously wander the house looking for him. In his letter of resignation he explained his decision:

> The decision was made, in a way, 42 years ago when
> I promised to care for Muriel "in sickness and in
> health . . . till death do us part." So . . . as a man
> of my word, integrity has something to do with it.
> But so does fairness. She has cared for me fully and
> sacrificially all these years; if I cared for her for the
> next 40 years I would not be out of her debt. Duty,
> however, can be grim and stoic. But there is more:
> I love Muriel. She is a delight to me—her childlike
> dependence and confidence in me, her warm love,
> occasional flashes of that wit I used to relish so, her
> happy spirit and tough resilience in the face of her
> continual distressing frustration. I don't *have* to

care for her. I *get* to! It is a high honor to care for so wonderful a person.[4]

It would have been hard to imagine, forty-two years before, when he stood with his young, beautiful bride at their wedding, exchanging their vows, that it would come to something like this. He said, "I mean back then, I hardly even heard the name [Alzheimer's]." But he had promised to love her no matter what, "in plenty and in want, in sickness and in health, in joy and in sorrow, as long as we both shall live."

A hardheaded man. The title of his book about his experience with Muriel's disease says it all: *A Promise Kept.* That's Ruth and Naomi; that's what it looks like. *"May the LORD punish me severely if I allow anything but death to separate us!"*

Lovable Samwise Gamgee is another hardheaded man, or rather a hardheaded hobbit, a fictional character in J. R. R. Tolkien's epic masterpiece series, The Lord of the Rings. Sam's friend Frodo has been given the awful task of destroying an evil and powerful ring by casting it into the Cracks of Doom in the dark and ghastly land of Mordor. Hobbits are tiny little creatures, homebodies, who love the quiet life of home and hearth, and who would choose a good meal and a mug of ale with good friends over an adventure anytime. On top of that, the chances are slim to none that Frodo will succeed in his task.

Gandalf, the wizard, knows how discouraged Frodo will get on this impossible journey. He will need a loyal friend to walk beside him, a hardheaded friend like Samwise Gamgee, to keep him going when he is ready to despair and give up. So Gandalf makes Samwise promise to go the distance with Frodo, to never leave him, no matter what. Other brave individuals will go too, but Sam has this special mission within the mission to Mordor. Nine will travel together in what they call "the Fellowship of the Ring."

"I MADE A PROMISE, MR. FRODO"

As the journey proceeds, things begin to unravel for the Fellowship as one mishap after another threatens their mission. All lives are in danger, and one life is lost, so Frodo makes a secret and brave decision to go it alone to prevent any further loss of life. At dusk, when no one is watching, he quietly slips away to a boat and pushes off from the shore of the river to quietly row to the other side and continue his trek to Mordor and the Cracks of Doom.

The following scene, as depicted in the film adaptation, is one of the most moving scenes in motion pictures. Frodo is halfway across the lake when he hears the loud snapping of branches and brush from the shore and sees the figure of his little hobbit companion, Sam Gamgee, running in his direction, frantically crying, "Frodo! Mr. Frodo!"

Frodo shouts, "Go back, Sam! I'm going to Mordor alone!"

But Sam continues barreling toward Frodo, now in the river up to his waist. "Of course you are. And I'm coming with you!"

"You can't swim!" Frodo shouts in horror. "Sam! Sam!"

Sam can't swim, but he will die trying. Gasping and coughing up water, Sam sinks beneath the gloomy surface of the river as Frodo reaches down and grabs his wrist, pulling him up and into the boat. Frodo looks at Sam incredulously, as if to say, *What are you thinking? Why would you risk your life for me?*

Wet and shivering, Sam sees the question in Frodo's eyes and says, "I made a promise, Mr. Frodo. A promise. 'Don't you leave him, Samwise Gamgee.' And I don't mean to. I don't mean to."

Frodo embraces Sam. "Come on then," he says, smiling.[5]

Again, that's the bond between Ruth and Naomi, lived out. "May the LORD punish me severely if I allow anything but death to separate us!"

Jesus said we must enter his Kingdom with the attitude and *agon* of an athlete or a warrior, the fierce determination to fight and run until the fight is finished and the race is run. Never is the *agon* of the Christian life more at work than in the commitments that require what Nietzsche called "a long obedience in the same direction." Christ's warrior-athletes know that the good life depends not on the number of experiences we have but on the strength and depth of our commitments.

HIS LOVE NEVER QUITS

Agon is hardheaded because God is hardheaded. Hardheaded love is the love that is most like God's love. Psalm 136 would be monotonous in its repetition were it not for glory of the phrase repeated. I like Eugene Peterson's rendering of it: "His love never quits." Over and over, one phrase after another, this psalm declares something about the greatness of God's love and always follows with the response—the same phrase twenty-six times!—"His love never quits." We are never more godly, or godlike, than when we keep our promises.

Marriages and families are sustained by hardheaded love. When I perform a wedding, I like to remind the couple and the congregation that at no time during the ceremony will I ask the bride or groom, "Do you love each other?" That's obvious. The critical question is not "do you?" but "will you love each other?" The marriage will be sustained over a lifetime, not by the things a couple decides to do in the mood of a moment, but by what they decide to do regardless of the mood or the moment. That's what McQuilkin meant when he said his decision to care for his wife had been made forty-two years before, when he made his promises.

We are never more godly, or godlike, than when we keep our promises.

I once heard a talk by writer Elisabeth Elliot in which she said, "Marriage is the institution for the preservation of love." At first I disagreed with her. I thought, *Isn't it the other way around? Isn't it being in love that makes the institution of marriage last?* But I've since discovered that it's the promise my bride and I made to keep on loving whether or not we're "in love" that has kept us in love over the last four decades. It's the structural, institutional side of life that makes the more personal and intimate side safe and possible. It's the confidence I have that my wife, Lauretta, will keep her promise to cherish me the way I am, no matter how unlovely I may be, that sets me free to actually become quite lovable. Just ask her!

MAKING PREDICTABLE THE UNPREDICTABLE

Hardheaded lovers do wonderful and powerful things. Lewis Smedes writes:

> They choose not to quit when the going gets rough because they promised once to see it through. They stick to lost causes. They hold on to a love grown cold. They stay with people who have become pains in the neck. They still dare to make promises and care enough to keep the promises they make. I want to say to you that if you have a ship you will not desert, if you have people you will not forsake, if you have causes you will not abandon, then *you are like God.*[6]

What a marvelous thing a promise is! When a person makes a promise, she reaches out into an unpredictable future and makes one thing predictable: she will be there even when being there costs her more than she wants to pay. When a person makes a promise, he stretches himself out into circumstances that no one can control and controls at least one thing: he will be there no matter what the circumstances turn out to be. With one simple word of promise, a person creates an island of certainty in a sea of uncertainty.

> **With one simple word of promise, a person creates an island of certainty in a sea of uncertainty.**

Or as Smedes says: "When a person makes a promise, she stakes a claim on her personal freedom and power. When you make a promise, you take a hand in creating your own future."[7]

But it's not only marriage and family that lives by this kind of love—it is everything we do in this world that is good and right.

In 1940, Clarence Jordan founded Koinonia Farm in Americus, Georgia, as the first interracial community in the South. After fourteen years of almost continuous intimidation and harassment, the Ku Klux Klan burned every building on the farm except Jordan's home.

In the midst of the raid, Jordan recognized a voice among the masked and hooded Klansmen. It was a voice he knew well—that of a local newspaper reporter. The reporter showed up the next day to do a story about the arson. He found Jordan in a field, planting seeds, while the rubble was still smoldering. With a barely discernible sneer in his voice, he said to Jordan, "I heard the awful news of your tragedy last night, and I came out to do a story on the closing of your farm."

Jordan kept planting and hoeing, as the reporter asked his

questions, poking and prodding, getting no response from Jordan. Frustrated, the reporter said, "You've got two PhDs, you've put fourteen years into this farm, and now there's nothing left. Just how successful do you think you've been?"

With that question, Jordan stopped hoeing and looked at his tormentor. He said, "About as successful as the cross.

"You just don't get it, do you? You don't understand us Christians. What we are about is not success, but faithfulness."[8]

God is the miracle worker, not you or I. All he asks of us is that we keep showing up and doing the right thing, faithfully, hardheadedly. Look at Ruth—in the darkest of times her faithful love shone like the light that shone in Bethlehem's dark streets centuries later; literally, almost. She became the great-grandmother of King David, whose greater Son would save us from our sins.

CHAPTER 19

COURAGE

THE VIRTUE THAT MAKES ALL THE OTHERS POSSIBLE

This is my command—be strong and courageous! Do not be afraid or discouraged. For the LORD your God is with you wherever you go.
JOSHUA 1:9

Courage is the first of human qualities because it is the quality that guarantees all others.
WINSTON CHURCHILL

THE GUARDIAN IS Mordecai, the ward is his cousin Esther, and the situation is desperate and dangerous. Their people, the Jews, are threatened with genocide, and the beautiful Esther, who has recently married the Persian despot Xerxes, appears to be their best chance for survival. Maybe she can influence her husband to head off the massacre. The conversation begins with Mordecai reminding Esther of the strategic place she occupies in the Persian Empire: "Who knows if perhaps you were made queen for just such a time as this?" (Esther 4:14).

True, very true, but it will still be dangerous for Esther. Xerxes is a tyrannical fool who doesn't like to be disturbed in his pursuit of pleasure. He might lose his hair-trigger temper and kill her if she brings her people's plight to him. She considers the danger but courageously determines to do whatever she can to save her people. She says, "If I must die, I must die" (v. 16).

YOU'VE GOT A PROBLEM

Esther's statement is a classic of courage. It's the kind of thing that inspired a Latin American evangelist who was arrested for preaching the gospel. When told he would be thrown in jail if he preached in that city again, he said, "No problem! I'll preach the gospel to all the prisoners and guards."

The magistrate turned red in the face and upped the stakes: "If you do that, I'll throw you into solitary confinement."

"No problem!" the evangelist answered. "Then I'll be alone with my Lord, and I'll pray for you."

"Then we'll have you executed!" the magistrate bellowed.

"No problem!" the evangelist exulted. "Then I'll be in heaven forever with my Lord."

Frustrated, the magistrate said to one of his henchmen, "What are we going to do with him?"

The evangelist said, "You've got a problem!"

There it is, the essence of courage: *If I must die, I must die.* I'll do whatever it takes to do the right thing. Courage is firmness of mind and strength of character in the face of difficulty or pain. Courage is not fearlessness, for there would be no need to be courageous if there were no fear. It is not fearlessness but the will to overcome fear for the sake of something more important than the fear, something of surpassing goodness.

Patrick Reardon says the difference between the courageous and the cowardly is "the difference between those who play it safe and those who play for keeps."[1] The cowardly look for the most they can get for the least investment; they come at life from the standpoint of a strict cost-benefit analysis in the immediate, the here and now. If it feels good, do it; if it doesn't feel good, or might not feel good, don't. The brave bet all they have on what is

> **Courage is not fearlessness but the will to overcome fear for the sake of something more important than the fear, something of surpassing goodness.**

best, even if it feels awful, even if they lose all they have. The brave are *in*, all the way in; the cowardly are never in, always on the edge, hedging their bets.

NO RESERVE! NO RETREAT! NO REGRETS!

Bill Borden was all the way in when he died of cerebral meningitis at age twenty-five. Born in 1887, the heir to the Borden dairy fortune, he was converted as a youth and went on to graduate from Yale University and attend Princeton Seminary. While a student, he came under the influence of the Student Volunteer Movement and the great Samuel Zwemer, known as "the apostle to Islam." When he was Borden's age, Zwemer declared that he wanted to take the gospel to the "hardest place on earth." Arabia fit that description, and off he went. Through people like Zwemer, Borden heard of the 15 million Muslims in northeast China, more

Muslims than in Egypt, Persia, or even Arabia, all without a gospel witness. He gave away his portion of the family fortune and went to Cairo to study Arabic. It was there that he got sick and died. Memorial services were held for him at Princeton and Yale, in New York, Chicago, Cairo, Japan, Korea, India, and South Africa. Borden may not have left behind many possessions, but he did leave a Bible in which he'd scrawled three memorable resolutions: "No Reserve! No Retreat! No Regrets!"[2] He was playing for keeps.

Courage is essential to the Christian life, for it is the "condition and catalyst"[3] of all the other virtues, the quality of soul that guarantees and makes all the others possible. Without courage, love and justice are empty ideals. Without courage to back them, they will wilt and fade in the face of opposition and danger. "For this reason," writes Patrick Reardon, "the man least deserving of our trust, on any matter whatever, is the coward."[4] Cowardice is to virtue what sterility is to pregnancy.

The Christian life is hard. It is an *agon*; persecution, hardship, and suffering go with the territory. You took sides in a war when you became a Christian—that requires courage. Jesus said it would be this way:

> *If you find the godless world is hating you, remember it*
> *got its start hating me. If you lived on the world's terms,*
> *the world would love you as one of its own. But since*
> *I picked you to live on God's terms and no longer on*
> *the world's terms, the world is going to hate you. When*

that happens, remember this: Servants don't get better treatment than their masters. If they beat on me, they will certainly beat on you. (John 15:18-20, *The Message*)

Paul identified courage in the face of hardship as one of the distinguishing marks of service to God. He said, "Yes, and everyone who wants to live a godly life in Christ Jesus will suffer persecution" (2 Timothy 3:12). He backed up this statement many times in his tumultuous apostolic career, but never more vividly than when he was stoned and left for dead in Lystra—yes, stoned; pummeled with rocks on the head and shoulders until dead. A freshly stoned corpse would be swollen and bruised and covered in blood. When the disciples gathered around him, presumably to bury him, he not only regained consciousness, he got up and traveled the next day to other churches in the region. He went to strengthen them and encourage them in the faith, "reminding them that we must suffer many hardships to enter the Kingdom of God" (Acts 14:22). Paul's face and body were his own sermon illustrations. Imagine him being introduced to the little congregations, the lacerations, bruises, and hematomas still on his face, an elder saying gravely, "Brother Paul has a few things to share with us today."

FACE ANOTHER DIRTY DIAPER?

Paul even included this stoning in his apostolic resume. Comparing his credentials to the so-called "super apostles" in

Corinth, with their impressive testimonies of mystical experience and spiritual power, Paul wrote:

> *I have worked harder, been put in prison more often, been whipped times without number, and faced death again and again. Five different times the Jewish leaders gave me thirty-nine lashes. Three times I was beaten with rods. Once I was stoned. Three times I was shipwrecked. Once I spent a whole night and a day adrift at sea. I have traveled on many long journeys. I have faced danger from rivers and from robbers. I have faced danger from my own people, the Jews, as well as from the Gentiles. I have faced danger in the cities, in the deserts, and on the seas. And I have faced danger from men who claim to be believers but are not. I have worked hard and long, enduring many sleepless nights. I have been hungry and thirsty and have often gone without food. I have shivered in the cold, without enough clothing to keep me warm.*
> (2 Corinthians 11:23-27)

What qualified him as an apostle were not his academic degrees and service record in the churches he pastored, nor his mystical experiences,[5] but the things he did that demanded courage.

This is all inspiring stuff, these stories of "the glorious company of apostles . . . the noble fellowship of prophets . . . the white-robed army of martyrs."[6] But the vast majority of Christians will never be called upon to be courageous in the

ways people like Esther, the Latin American evangelist, Bill
Borden, and Paul were.

One afternoon as my wife, Lauretta, and I were sipping
tea together, discussing the lives of the martyrs, she blurted
out, "I'm pretty sure that if I were given the choice whether
to deny my faith or stand before a firing squad, I'd face the
bullets. The hard part right now is facing another dirty dia-
per. Sometimes it seems harder to live for Christ than to die
for him." We had several small children in our family at the
time, and the grind of daily work was endless. As refreshing
as the tea was, it added to our sense of numbing triviality.
I remembered reading somewhere of a pastor who com-
plained, "Wherever Paul went there was a riot; wherever I
go, they serve tea."

A CHOREOGRAPHY IN THESE COINCIDENCES

Courage is not defined by the drama of the challenge but by
faithfulness in whatever the challenge is; whether death by
sword or cancer, a bad marriage or a lousy job, or committee
meetings. In the biblical lexicon,
faithfulness and courage are virtually synonymous. Whatever the
occasions for courage may be—and
they are innumerable—it is always
fed by the same sources.

> In the biblical lexicon,
> faithfulness and courage
> are virtually synonymous.

The first is the confidence that God is in charge of history, on all levels, micro and macro, the trivial and the

monumental; that not a hair falls from our heads, or an emperor from a throne, without the will of our Father in heaven; and that this same Father works in all things for the good of those who love him and are called according to his purpose. There can be no random events, no accidents with this God, for all things must serve his good purposes for us.

Esther said, "If I must die, I must die." But wait, God is not mentioned even once in the book of Esther. What are we to make of that? That is the genius of the book. Read it: though threatened with genocide, the Jews seem to be the luckiest people on earth when the story is over. How lucky for them that Esther was such a gorgeous woman. How fortunate that she beat the other women out in the Bride-for-Xerxes competition and won the king's confidence. How lucky for them that Mordecai just happened to overhear an assassination plot. Coincidences collect, one upon another, and lo! the evil Haman, the proto-Hitler, ends up falling in the pit he dug for others.[7]

But maybe the Jews are just a little too lucky, like the suspicious character who keeps beating the house in roulette. Maybe there is some manipulation of the game going on somewhere. To paraphrase a line by songwriter David Wilcox, there is a *choreography in these coincidences*.[8] That is the point of a story in which the main character, God, isn't mentioned because that is the way he carries out so much of his governance of the world: incognito, choreographing coincidences, working quietly behind the scenes. Or maybe it's the other way around; as Chesterton suggested, *maybe we are the ones behind the scenes.* Maybe we are looking at the world from behind, and if we could get in front we would meet, face-to-face, the smiling Providence who is so hidden.

People who believe this can abandon themselves to divine providence, as Jean-Pierre de Caussade counseled, and discover a sacramental quality in each moment, no matter how vexing or mundane.[9] Call it hope. Call it the sovereignty of God. Whatever you call it, it will give you courage.

The second source of courage, ironically, is fear—or rather, fearing what you should, and not fearing what you shouldn't. Jesus tells us

> People who abandon themselves to divine providence discover a sacramental quality in each moment, no matter how vexing or mundane.

how to tell which is which: "Dear friends, don't be afraid of those who want to kill your body; they cannot do any more to you after that. But I'll tell you whom to fear. Fear God, who has the power to kill you and then throw you into hell. Yes, he's the one to fear" (Luke 12:4-5).

MEN WITHOUT CHESTS

Bad fear: fearing those who can only kill your body, or make your life miserable or uncomfortable, but can do nothing more. Good fear: fearing God, the one who can not only kill your body but also throw you into hell. But here is the beauty and inexpressible comfort of good fear: good fear casts out bad fear. "What is the price of five sparrows—two copper coins? Yet God does not forget a single one of them. And the very hairs on your head are all numbered. So don't be afraid; you are more valuable to God than a whole flock of sparrows" (Luke 12:6-7).

Fear God, and you'll need not fear him—or anything or anybody—anymore! The fear of the Lord is not only the beginning of wisdom but of courage, too. We must not fear mere fear—but the wrong kind of fear. For God's "unfailing love toward those who *fear* him is as great as the height of the heavens above the earth. . . . The Lord is like a father to his children, tender and compassionate to those who *fear* him. For he knows how weak we are. . . . The love of the Lord remains forever with those who *fear* him" (Psalm 103:11, 13-14, 17, italics mine).

Irony, truly. The one who will not submit to evil is the one who has first submitted to God. Those most to be reckoned with, most to be feared, are those who will not back down, not submit in the face of danger and discouragement, because they have first submitted to the will of God. They have declared from the depths of their being, "Your law, O God, is written on my heart!"[10]

Our English word *courage* comes from the French word for *heart*. Since the heart is what pumps blood and oxygen to the whole body, it's a wonderful metaphor for what gives the strength to overcome the trials and hateful threats of our enemies. To have a strong heart is to have courage; to lose heart is to lose courage.

In *The Abolition of Man*, C. S. Lewis spoke of "men

without chests."[11] He was drawing on an ancient anthropology that had the faculty of ideas and thought residing in the head, feelings and sentiment in the belly, and virtue and moral courage in the chest. We are a culture that abounds with ideas and emotions, intellect, and feelings but that has scant supply of virtue and moral courage. We doubt that such things as virtue and morality can even be known. What a grotesque picture! There is no chest. The belly is bloated and gaseous, the head is swollen and teetering precariously atop a skinny little chest. No wonder we are so afraid and confused. No wonder we medicate and divert ourselves. No wonder we cannot stand straight.

IS THAT ALL?

Jesus had a chest in the garden of Gethsemane. He certainly felt the terror of the Cross and, worse, the hellish separation from his Father that would come with it. No doubt he had thought of the satanic alternative. He threw himself on the ground and cried, "Abba! Father! Is there any other way?" Three times he did this. Sweat fell from his body like drops of blood. But his heart and his Father's heart were one. To that holy courage we owe our eternal salvation.

When my eldest son, Dan, was seven or eight, he came bursting into the cabin we were staying in at Forest Home Christian Conference Center. I was there to speak at a conference and had brought my little family with me. My wife and I had met there many years ago as part of the summer staff of 1970. I had spent many hours in the prayer chapel there praying about all the kinds of things a young man like me prayed about. My prayers were full of uncertainty and yearning. Danny had discovered the prayer chapel, and he wanted to show it to me. "Dad! There's a little cabin where people pray!" he said. "You want to see it?"

Of course I did, and as the little boy who represented so many of the kinds of things I prayed about in those years led me down the path to the chapel, I marveled at God's faithfulness. My future was leading me back to my past.

We entered the chapel and sat down. Our conversation was in whispers. He asked me about the window in the back, a stained glass depiction of Jesus praying in Gethsemane.

"Is that Jesus, Daddy?"

"It is," I answered.

"Is he praying?"

"He is, son."

"What's he praying about?"

How do you explain that to a little boy?

I said, "He's telling his Father that he will do whatever he asks him to do."

Danny thought for a moment and asked, "Is that all, Daddy?"

"Yes," I said, "that is all."

I remember that I had my arm over his shoulder, and my hand was on his heart.

CHAPTER 20

FINISHING WELL

LET ME GET HOME BEFORE DARK

That is why we never give up. Though our bodies are dying, our spirits are being renewed every day. For our present troubles are small and won't last very long. Yet they produce for us a glory that vastly outweighs them and will last forever! So we don't look at the troubles we can see now; rather, we fix our gaze on things that cannot be seen. For the things we see now will soon be gone, but the things we cannot see will last forever.
2 CORINTHIANS 4:16-18

Few, they tell me, finish well. . . . Lord, let me get home before dark.
ROBERTSON MCQUILKIN, *A PROMISE KEPT*

AT 7 P.M. on October 7, 1968, the last few thousand spectators were filing out of the Mexico City Olympics Stadium. Night was approaching, and the temperature had cooled. More than an hour earlier, Mamo Wolde of Ethiopia had won the gold medal in the marathon, looking as strong at the end of the 26-mile, 385-yard race as he had at the beginning. A few stragglers in the race were being assisted at first aid stations, when the familiar police sirens and whistles blared once more though the gate of the stadium. There was one more runner entering the track, John Stephen Akhwari of Tanzania, the last-place finisher, limping, his leg bandaged and bloody. He had a bad fall earlier in the race, and now all he could do was grimace and hobble around the last lap as the crowd cheered and applauded his courage.

Later he was asked, "You are badly injured. Why didn't you quit? Why didn't you give up?"

Akhwari answered softly and with dignity: "My country did not send me five thousand miles to start this race. My country sent me to finish."

My guess is, if anyone remembers what happened in the 1968 Olympic marathon, the name Akhwari is remembered as much as Wolde, probably more. Each, in his own way, was triumphant; each won a kind of victory. More than winning a medal, it is the courage and sacrifice of the struggle that captures our imaginations and thrills our hearts. Great athletic ability is a genetic gift, not an achievement. It's not what you were given that makes for greatness; it's what you do with what you were given. Great ability is not a moral quality; great courage and determination are. But even these are gifts from God, evidences of his grace at work in us.[1]

Great ability is not a moral quality; great courage and determination are.

IT'S THE FINISHING THAT MATTERS

When Paul wrote at the end of his life, "I have fought the good fight, I have finished the race, and I have remained faithful" (2 Timothy 4:7), was he charging across the finish line like Mamo Wolde, or was he limping like John Stephen

Akhwari? We don't know, of course. And what would charging or limping look like spiritually? I have some ideas, but I'm convinced that it's the finishing that matters. All Paul says is that he went the distance and fought the fight and finished the race, and that he didn't desert or drop out.

Along the way Paul was afflicted with so bad a "thorn" in his flesh that he begged God to take it away, to remove a personal weakness so great that it tormented and humiliated him. All he got from God was a gracious refusal and a promise: "My grace is all you need. My power works best in weakness" (2 Corinthians 12:9). So Paul remained "weak" for the rest of his life, even as God showed the riches of his grace in him.

What did Paul look like, how bold and triumphant did he seem, when (as tradition has it) he knelt outside the gates of Rome, bared his neck, and was beheaded? I would like to think that he still had as much grit and chutzpah as he and Silas had years before as they sat singing hymns, locked in the stocks of a Philippian prison, their backs raw from a scourging. I don't know, and I don't think it matters, because all that ultimately matters is that he went the distance, fought the fight and finished the race, didn't desert and didn't drop out.

In his great resurrection manifesto Paul wrote, "Our bodies are buried in brokenness, but they will be raised in glory. They are buried in weakness, but they will be raised in strength" (1 Corinthians 15:43). How true.

My elderly friend says he wants to finish his life the way the running great Jim Ryun finished his races. Ryun, who was the first high school athlete to break the four-minute barrier in the mile, was famous for his "kicks" at the end of a race; in many races he would be at the back of the pack, but his final sprint over the last two hundred yards won a lot of contests. My friend wants to end with a heroic flourish, vigorous and upbeat in spirit. But he has chronic severe back pain, and he has always been prone to depression. When I was a lot younger I might have judged him spiritually weak. If he had asked me for advice back then, I would have counseled him to pray more, get his head straight, and buck up and live like a man. I see things differently now. A cheery finish is not likely for my friend, but a faithful finish, even a joyful one, is.

In the eyes of Christ, our Righteous Judge, Akhwari will be as good as Wolde in the end. How can that be? Because our righteousness is Christ's righteousness, not our own, from start to finish. Otherwise muscular faith would be reduced to just another form of works-righteousness.

THE SAME GRACE THAT SAVES US PRESERVES US

Then there was my dear friend, my buddy, my partner in the good fight—as courageous and faithful a warrior as I have ever known. He battled and overcame multiple learning deficiencies, mood disorders, and weird biochemical issues to not only finish college and seminary but to write a book about his struggles. He wrote to encourage others who have the same challenges. The church he pastored was proud of him, his friends adored and trusted him, and the poor were blessed by his generosity. He was an amazing combination of humility and moral toughness. He was a great husband and father who treasured his wife and kids. Oh yes, and he was really good-looking.

In February 2010 he took his life.

Inexplicably, the things he had battled for so long seemed to gather strength, and a depression deeper than any he had ever known descended upon him. He just couldn't fight his way out of it. God knows he tried—if ever I have doubted that depression can be a deadly disease, I doubt it no longer. The man fought hard. I'll never forget the terror in his eyes as we talked and prayed and he tried so hard to feel what he believed was true. He wanted to hang on, but one day, in what I believe was an impulsive moment of panic and despair, he committed suicide.

God! I miss him!

The questions of why these things can happen to even the best of us are too many, too murky, and too difficult to address here. But what I want to be absolutely clear on is that my friend ran a hard race and fought a good fight, and while he didn't finish like Wolde, he came to the end and stumbled and fell with all the anguished courage of Akhwari. And the same grace that saved him when he trusted Christ as a boy saved him at the end.

I have no guarantees exactly how good my finish will be, or whether I will even have sufficient possession of my faculties to care. My hope is not in how well I will perform at the end but in the power of my faithful Savior and Shepherd to lead and love me safely through the end. My hope is in him. But since I am living in the "end times" of my life—always have, actually, but I was too dumb to realize it—and because the Bible commands us to "realize the brevity of life, so that we may grow in wisdom" (Psalm 90:12), I have been rehearsing the finish, practicing certain qualities I believe will nourish my life in Christ now and at the end.

YEARNING

I want to live out my days yearning for more of God. It's a cliché, but I don't want to settle into a faith that is comfortable and predictable. I pray the Holy Spirit will stir me up with the kind of holy dissatisfaction that will move me to "press on to possess that perfection for which Christ Jesus first possessed me," to fight "to reach the end of the race and receive the heavenly prize for which God, through Christ Jesus, is calling us" (Philippians 3:12, 14). For God is a God of the future, always a step ahead, out on the edge of the horizon, beckoning and urging us to follow him into strange and wonder-full places.

When he was in his sixties, Karl Barth protested the inertia that works like sludge in the soul—at any time of life, but especially near the end—and that tempts us to freeze in our call to go where Christ commands and to grasp that perfection for which Christ first grasped us. He used the vivid image of a river rushing to the falls to encourage those nearing the end of life to press on: "As if it were permissible to freeze or solidify at the point where the river of responsibility should flow more torrentially than ever in view of the approaching falls, of the proximity of the coming Judge!"[2]

I don't want to be afraid to get in over my head and to go way beyond my abilities with God. I want to be like Abraham and Sarah, who heard God's call when Abraham was seventy-five years old, who had their first child, Isaac, when Abraham was ninety-nine and an adolescent in their household when they were well into their hundreds! Now, I don't particularly want that very thing, mind you, but I don't want to be afraid of it.

I want to be like the bachelor pastor Dr. Charles McCoy, who was forced into retirement when he turned seventy-two because the church he had pastored for decades thought he was too old to do it anymore. At first he was crushed, a pastor being put out to pasture; but after a lot of prayer, he responded to a call to go to India to be an itinerant evangelist. When he told the church board his plans, they were aghast. "But what if you die in India?" the concerned elders wanted to know. His answer was, "It's as close to heaven from India as it is from here."

And it was closer to Jesus than where he was, because India was where Jesus wanted to take him. Thus began a ministry that did not end until he died in his sleep during an afternoon nap when he was eighty-eight. Going to heaven while taking an afternoon nap! What a pleasure to go from one delight (an afternoon nap) to the greatest delight of all,

245

the presence of God; to experience fully what he had long believed about God: "You will show me the way of life, granting me the joy of your presence and the pleasures of living with you forever" (Psalm 16:11).

MARVELING

I want to keep marveling at what a wondrous thing it is to be alive in this astonishing world, living under the watchful care of my Father. That will mean getting smaller as I get older. G. K. Chesterton told a parable about a little boy who was magically given the choice to be big or small. Predictably the boy chose to be made gigantic, so big he could stride across North America in minutes, or kick over Mount Everest like a sand castle. It was fun to be a giant for a while, but it soon got lonely. There was no one to play with, and the world seemed as mundane and boring as his backyard. He was miserable being so big. But if he had chosen instead to be tiny, so tiny that his backyard would be like the Amazon rain forest to him, the mud puddle like Lake Superior, he would never have run out of wonders to behold. He could have spent a lifetime happily exploring his neighborhood.

Annie Dillard writes:

An infant who has just learned to hold his head up has a frank and forthright way of gazing about him in bewilderment. He hasn't the faintest clue where he is, and he aims to learn. In a couple of years, what he will have learned instead is how to fake it: he'll have the cocksure air of a squatter who has come to feel he owns the place.[3]

Small is good, because small means being humble—*childlike.* And childlike is good because only the humble can see things as they are and be thankful and amazed and blessed by God. Only the humble can come near God, because God opposes the proud (the big) and favors the humble (the little ones).[4] One day, as Jesus got to thinking about this, he became ecstatic and "was filled with the joy of the Holy Spirit." He prayed, "O Father, Lord of heaven and earth, thank you for hiding these things from those who think themselves wise and clever, and for revealing them to the childlike. Yes, Father, it pleased you to do it this way" (Luke 10:21).

> Only the humble can see things as they are and be thankful and amazed and blessed by God.

In the same way, I want to be small enough to be delighted with the things that sent Jesus into ecstasy. I want to go to the end amazed that one such as I was so graced to be able to see the things that the angels in heaven eagerly watch.[5]

HOPING DEFIANTLY

I want to keep hoping. If it is true that hope is hearing the melody of the future, and faith is to dance to it, then I want to keep tapping my foot till the end.[6] Death is the last enemy, but it won't have the last word. No matter how worn and weary my body and spirit may get, I want to hope defiantly that when I die, that won't be the last you'll see of me; that when I see Christ as he is, I will at long last be as he is. The Bible says I will.[7]

My friend Dave Hopkins had his life cut short by multiple sclerosis. Little by little, this gifted musician and worship leader lost all muscular control until he could no longer sing or breathe. He fought the disease for years with diet and medical maneuverings, and he was able, for quite a while, to sit in a wheelchair and strum simple chords on his guitar as he led singing. One evening he was leading us in a gospel chorus that had us singing things like, "When the Lord says pray, I will pray," or "When the Lord says sing, I will sing," or "When the Lord says preach, I will preach"— things like that. The last verse was, "When the Lord says *dance*, I will *dance*." Dave sang it defiantly, with a twinkle in his eye. We sang it with tears in ours. We were all singing with poet John Donne, who wrote:

> *If it is true that hope is hearing the melody of the future, and faith is to dance to it, then I want to keep tapping my foot till the end.*

> *Death be not proud, though some have called thee*
> *Mighty and dreadful, for, thou art not so,*
> *For, those, whom thou think'st, thou dost overthrow,*
> *Die not, poor death, nor yet canst thou kill me. . . .*

One short sleep past, we wake eternally,
And death shall be no more; death, thou shalt die.[8]

I love the mockery in that last line, "death, thou shalt die." Donne got it from Paul (who got it from Hosea), who taunted death:

O death, where is your victory?
O death, where is your sting? (1 Corinthians 15:55)

I attended a lecture on how children face death. The speaker showed us a picture drawn by a small child with terminal cancer, which pictured death as a massive tank. It consumed nearly all of the paper, and its giant gun barrel was leveled at the head of the child, who was holding up a little sign, with even smaller letters, that spelled "Stop." It was heartwrenching to see. I would have loved to see the words on the sign read, "You want some of this? Bring it on. Death, you bloated, blustering bully, *you're* gonna die." I may hope in that way—it is permitted—and I pray that I will face death with that resolve.

LET ME GET HOME BEFORE DARK

But a caveat: Death, be not proud and, Ben, you be not proud either. Any defiance I can muster against death is, truth be told, a little bluster too. I cringe at what death will do to me, even fear it. Death isn't the last word, but as next-to-last-words go, it's pretty scary. So I want to finish running and walking, or limping, in the comfort and love of the One who loved me so many years ago, who knocked on my heart's door asking entrance. Mrs. Dalton's "Good News" club was where I first heard the gospel of God's love and memorized the first Bible verse I ever memorized, John 3:16, King James Version:

> *For God so loved the world, that he gave his only begotten Son, that whosoever believeth in him should not perish, but have everlasting life.*

It was love that drew me to God: rich, extravagant, undeserved, unasked-for love. It has been faithful love that has kept me in the struggle and love that will get me across the finish line and home.

I have failed him so many times that I can make no demands and claim no rights to his mercy. And whatever service I offer, I offer because he first served and keeps on serving me. I am so ashamed of my misdeeds and my callous heart that I sometimes want to either hide from his face or work so hard to serve him that I can offset the weight of guilt I have piled up. But he will have none of it. He is always glad to see me, always ready to pick me up and clean me up. It was for joy (!) that he suffered the shame and agony of the Cross

Faithful love has kept me in the struggle, and love will get me across the finish line and home.

in my place. So I blush and thank him, and ask again, for the millionth time, that he forgive and restore me, that he strengthen me to finish the race and fight the good fight. And I will live to end in the confidence that the "one who judges [me] most finally will be the one who loves [me] most fully."[9]

And I will keep praying for the grace to finish well and with honor. I will pray for myself the kind of prayer Robertson McQuilkin prayed for himself:

It's sundown, Lord. The shadows of my life stretch back into the dimness of the years long spent. I fear not death, for that grim foe betrays himself at last, thrusting me forever into life: Life with you, unsoiled and free. But I do fear. I fear the Dark Specter may come too soon—or do I mean too late? That I should end before I finish or finish, but not well. That I should stain your honor, shame your name, grieve your loving heart. Few, they tell me, finish well. . . . Lord, let me get home before dark.[10]

ENDNOTES

INTRODUCTION: A FAITH WORTH FIGHTING FOR

1. From my book *Serving God: The Grand Essentials of Work and Worship* (Downers Grove, IL: InterVarsity Press, 1994), 126–127.
2. Quoted by Paul Johnson, *A History of Christianity* (New York: Atheneum, 1980), 4.
3. C. S. Lewis, *The Weight of Glory and Other Addresses* (Grand Rapids, MI: William B. Eerdmans Publishing Company, 1977), 12.
4. Dietrich Bonhoeffer, *The Cost of Discipleship* (New York: The Macmillan Company, 1964), 31.

CHAPTER 1: THE CALL

1. Gerhard Kittel, ed., *Theological Dictionary of the New Testament,* vol. 1, trans. Geoffrey W. Bromiley (Grand Rapids, MI: William B. Eerdmans Publishing Company, 1964), 134–140.
2. Bradley Nassif writes, "Grace is opposed to merit, but it is not opposed to effort." "The Poverty of Love" in *Christianity Today,* May 2008, 37.
3. Paul Lee Tan, *Encyclopedia of 7700 Illustrations* (Rockville, MD: Assurance Publishers, 1984), illustration number 5397.
4. Augustine, *The Confessions,* Book X, 29, 40, trans. Maria Boulding, O.S.B. (Hyde Park, NY: New City Press, 1997), 263.
5. As the apostle Paul said, "Oh, my dear children! I feel as if I'm going through labor pains for you again, and they will continue until Christ is fully developed in your lives" (Galatians 4:19).

CHAPTER 2: THE GOD WHO CALLS

1. Peter Kreeft, *How to Win the Culture War* (Downers Grove, IL: InterVarsity Press, 2002), 19.
2. Tremper Longman III and Daniel G. Reid, *God Is a Warrior* (Grand Rapids, MI: Zondervan Publishing House, 1995), 9. I consider this the seminal book on God as warrior and borrowed it for the subtitle of this chapter.
3. Eugene Peterson, *The Contemplative Pastor: Returning to the Art of Spiritual Direction* (Grand Rapids, MI: William B. Eerdmans Publishing Company, 1993), 30.
4. John White, *The Fight* (Downers Grove, IL: InterVarsity Press, 1976), 216.
5. See Romans 8:34.
6. See 1 Corinthians 1:24-25.
7. Tom Clancy attributes this quote to Orwell in his novel *The Teeth of the Tiger*.

CHAPTER 3: DON'T TRY THIS ALONE

1. C. S. Lewis, *The Screwtape Letters* (New York: HarperCollins, 2001 edition), 118.
2. An idea advanced in C. S. Lewis's book *The Weight of Glory*.
3. Peter Kreeft, *Christianity for Modern Pagans* (San Francisco: Ignatius Press, 1993), 322.
4. Quoted by Ben Patterson, *He Has Made Me Glad* (Downers Grove, IL: InterVarsity Press, 2005), 100.
5. David Zimmerman, *Deliver Us From Me-Ville* (Colorado Springs: David C. Cook, 2008).

CHAPTER 4: THE WAR

1. White, *The Fight*, 216.
2. Peter Berger, "For a World with Windows" in *Against the World for the World*, ed. P. Berger and R. J. Neuhaus (New York: Seabury Press, 1976), 10.
3. N. T. Wright, "What Is This Word?" in *Christianity Today*, December 21, 2006, http://www.christianitytoday.com/ct/2006/decemberweb-only/151-42.0.html.
4. Words from the Christmas carol "Away in a Manger."
5. Most folks define conflict as "Somebody is causing me to feel bad." Speed Leas in *Leadership* 10, no. 1.
6. James I. Packer, *A Quest for Godliness* (Wheaton, IL: Crossway Books, 1990), 22–23.

CHAPTER 5: THE STAKES

1. Quoted by Kreeft in *Christianity for Modern Pagans*, 142.
2. Blaise Pascal, *Pensees*, trans. A. J. Krailsheimer (New York: Penguin Books, 1983), number 133.
3. Peter Kreeft, *Three Philosophies of Life* (San Francisco: Ignatius Press, 1989), 61.
4. Pascal, *Pensees*, number 166.
5. Ibid., number 199.
6. C. J. Mahaney and Robin Boisvert, *How Can I Change? Victory in the Struggle Against Sin* (Gaithersburg, MD: Sovereign Grace Ministries, 1993), 86–90.
7. Clifton Fadiman, ed., *The Little, Brown Book of Anecdotes* (Boston: Little, Brown and Company, 1985), 543:7.
8. C. S. Lewis, *God in the Dock* (Grand Rapids, MI: William B. Eerdmans Publishing Company, 1970), 243–244.
9. Quoted by C. S. Lewis in *George MacDonald: An Anthology* (New York: The MacMillan Company, 1948), 19.
10. Lewis, *The Weight of Glory*, 5, 15.

CHAPTER 6: THE URGENCY

1. M. Scott Peck, *The Road Less Traveled* (New York: Touchstone, 1978), 15.
2. Bruce Thielemann, "Tide Riding," *Preaching Today* no. 30; submitted by Kevin A. Miller, Wheaton, IL.

CHAPTER 7: THE PRIZE

1. Ernest Shackleton, Frank Hurley, and Fergus Fleming, *South: The Endurance Expedition* (London: William Heinemann, 1919; London: Penguin Books, 2002), 200. Citations refer to the Penguin edition.
2. C. S. Lewis, "Christian Apologetics" in *God in the Dock* (Grand Rapids, MI: William B. Eerdmans Publishing Company, 1994), 101.
3. C. S. Lewis, "What Are We to Make of Jesus Christ?" in *God in the Dock* (Grand Rapids, MI: William B. Eerdmans Publishing Company, 1994), 158.
4. Augustine, *The Confessions*, Book I, trans. R. S. Pine-Coffin (London: Penguin Classics, 1961), 21.
5. A memorable image, attributed to Pascal.
6. C. S. Lewis, *The Weight of Glory* (New York: HarperCollins, 1949), 36.
7. See 1 John 3:3.
8. Lewis, *The Weight of Glory*, 1–2.

9. Quoted by John Piper in *The Roots of Endurance* (Wheaton, IL: Crossway Books, 2002), 68.

CHAPTER 8: THE FOOL

1. See John 10:9, KJV; Revelation 3:7.
2. C. L. Null, Oklahoma City, Oklahoma, qtd. in "Kids of the Kingdom," *Christian Reader.*
3. My thanks to Oswald Chambers for this apt and memorable phrase.
4. William Wilberforce, *Real Christianity: Discerning True Faith from False Beliefs*, ed. James M. Houston, fourth edition (Colorado Springs, CO: David C. Cook, 2005), 133.
5. *Chariots of Fire* (Warner Brothers, 1981), written by Colin Welland, directed by Hugh Hudson; submitted by Greg Asimakoupoulos and Doug Scott as illustration for *Preaching Today*. Italics mine.

CHAPTER 9: THE COST

1. To see this image, go to http://www.warnersallman.com/collection/images/head-of-christ/.
2. "My Song Is Love Unknown," in *Hymns II*, ed. Paul Beckwith, Hughes M. Huffman, and Mark Hunt (Downers Grove, IL: InterVarsity Press, 1976), 61.
3. C. S. Lewis, *The Problem of Pain* (New York: Touchstone Books, 1996), 45.
4. Ibid., 41.
5. See 2 Corinthians 5:17.
6. Quoted by Kreeft in *Fundamentals of the Faith* (San Francisco; Ignatius Press, 1988), 194. Also quoted by C. S. Lewis in *Mere Christianity*, chapter 9.
7. See John 1:11-13.
8. See John 1:1-4; Colossians 1:15-17.
9. See Isaiah 55:11.

CHAPTER 10: DISAPPOINTMENT WITH GOD

1. This phrase was coined by Os Guinness.
2. This is how Eugene Peterson renders it in *The Message*.
3. Both the Luther and Sibbes quotes are from Donald Bloesch, *The Struggle of Prayer* (New York: Harper and Row, 1980), 91, 93.
4. Frederick Buechner, *Wishful Thinking: A Theological ABC* (New York: Harper and Row, 1973), 25, italics mine.

PART 4: THE ESSENTIALS
1. Ian Ker, *G. K. Chesterton: A Biography* (New York: Oxford, 2011), 267.

CHAPTER 11: PERSISTENT PRAYER
1. This is one of the best-known lines from Lily Tomlin's one-woman show, *The Search for Signs of Intelligent Life in the Universe.*
2. George Buttrick, *Prayer* (Nashville: Abingdon-Cokesbury, 1942), 59.
3. The entire story is recorded in Matthew 15:21-28.
4. C. S. Lewis, *A Grief Observed* (New York: HarperCollins, 1961), 17–18.
5. Helmut Thielicke expands on this in his book *The Silence of God.*
6. Kreeft, *Three Philosophies of Life*, 61.
7. To read these stories, see Luke 11:5-10; 18:1-8.
8. P. T. Forsyth, *The Soul of Prayer* (Vancouver: Regent College Publishing, 1916), 104.
9. Ibid., 109.

CHAPTER 12: PATIENT PRAYER
1. Basil Miller, *George Muller, Man of Faith and Miracles* (Minneapolis: Bethany House Publishers, 1983), 145–146.
2. Ibid., 146, italics in the original.
3. Quoted in Basil Miller, *Mary Slessor* (Minneapolis: Bethany House Publishers, 1974), 130, 138.
4. Andrew Murray, *With Christ in the School of Prayer* (New Kensington, PA: Whitaker House, 1985), 236.
5. Studs Terkel, *Working* (New York: Pantheon Books, 1972), xi.
6. "Apostles' Creed," the Lutheran Church Missouri Synod, accessed March 30, 2011, http://www.lcms.org/Document.fdoc?src=lcm&id=954.

CHAPTER 13: JOY
1. See Ephesians 3:14-21.
2. Karl Barth, "The Doctrine of Reconciliation IV.1," in *Church Dogmatics* (Edinburgh: T. and T. Clark, 1980), 41.
3. George Herbert, "Gratefulness," in *The Complete English Works*, ed. Ann Pasternak Slater (New York: Everyman's Library, 1995), 120–121.
4. Quoted by Robert Llewelyn in *Our Duty and Our Joy* (London: Darton, Longman and Todd, 1993), 1; from chapter 15 of William Law, *A Serious Call to a Devout and Holy Life.*
5. Virginia Stem Owens, *And the Trees Clap Their Hands*, quoted by Bob Benson and Michael W. Benson in *Disciplines for the Inner Life* (Waco, TX: Word Books, 1985), 334.

6. From R. C. Sproul, "We've Grown Accustomed to His Grace," *Preaching Today* Tape No. 88 (Carol Steam, IL: *Christianity Today*, 1990).
7. Os Guinness, *God in the Dark* (Wheaton, IL: Crossway, 1996), 43.

CHAPTER 14: HOPE

1. Paul detailed the price he paid for his service to God in 2 Corinthians 11:23-27. He wrote, "[I have] been whipped times without number, and faced death again and again. Five different times the Jewish leaders gave me thirty-nine lashes. Three times I was beaten with rods. Once I was stoned. Three times I was shipwrecked. Once I spent a whole night and a day adrift at sea. I have traveled on many long journeys. I have faced danger from rivers and from robbers. I have faced danger from my own people, the Jews, as well as from the Gentiles. I have faced danger in the cities, in the deserts, and on the seas. And I have faced danger from men who claim to be believers but are not. I have worked hard and long, enduring many sleepless nights. I have been hungry and thirsty and have often gone without food. I have shivered in the cold, without enough clothing to keep me warm."
2. A phrase of Friedrich Nietsche's and used to great effect in a book by the same name: Eugene Peterson, *A Long Obedience in the Same Direction*.
3. Rubem Alves, *Tomorrow's Child: Imagination, Creativity, and the Rebirth of Culture* (New York: Harper and Row, 1972), 195.
4. Leith Anderson, *Leadership That Works* (Minneapolis: Bethany House, 1999), 164–165.
5. William Cowper, "God Moves in a Mysterious Way," in *The Hymnal* (Philadelphia: Presbyterian Board of Christian Education, 1933), 103.
6. Quoted by John Piper in *The Roots of Endurance* (Wheaton, IL: Crossway Books, 2002), 57.
7. Lewis, *The Weight of Glory*, 14.

CHAPTER 15: SABBATH

1. See Genesis 1:1–2:3.
2. Julian of Norwich as quoted in *Devotional Classics*, ed. Richard J. Foster and James Bryan Smith (San Francisco: HarperSanFrancisco, 1993), 68.

CHAPTER 16: MORTIFICATION OF SIN

1. White, *The Fight*, 216.
2. From *Pogo*, the famous comic strip (1948–1975) created by Walt Kelly and set in the Okefenokee Swamp of Georgia.
3. See Revelation 12:10; John 8:44; 1 John 3:8.

4. Charles H. Kraft, *Defeating Dark Angels* (Ventura, CA: Regal, 1992), 78.

5. John Owen, *Sin and Temptation* (Grand Rapids, MI: Bethany House, 1996). Reprinted as *Triumph over Temptation: Pursuing a Life of Purity*, ed. James M. Houston (Colorado Springs, CO: Cook, 2005), 133. Citations refer to the Cook edition.

6. C. S. Lewis, *Surprised by Joy* (New York: Harcourt, Brace and World, 1955), 226.

7. George Herbert, "The Reprisal," *The Complete English Works*, ed. Ann Pasternak Slater (New York: Everyman's Library, Alfred A. Knopf), 33.

8. Thomas Kelly in his William Penn Lecture "Holy Obedience" at Haverford College, Philadelphia, in 1939. See also Psalm 2:1-2.

9. Andrée Seu, "The Active Heart," *World*, August 23/30 2008, 87.

CHAPTER 17: LEARNING TO LOVE THE GOOD

1. *Renovation of the Heart* is the title of Dallas Willard's important book on the Christian life. Its subtitle says it all: "Putting on the Character of Christ."

2. C. S. Lewis, *Mere Christianity* (New York: HarperCollins, 1952), 56–57, italics in the original.

3. Buechner, *Wishful Thinking*, 79.

4. Lewis, *The Weight of Glory*, 15.

5. C. S. Lewis, *The Screwtape Letters* (New York: The Macmillan Company, 1944), 45–46.

6. Dante, *The Divine Comedy*, canto 33 (Chicago: Houghton Mifflin Company, 1952), 157.

7. My paraphrase of Ezekiel 20:43 and 36:31. Ezekiel 36:28-31 reads, "And you will live in Israel, the land I gave your ancestors long ago. You will be my people, and I will be your God. I will cleanse you of your filthy behavior. I will give you good crops of grain, and I will send no more famines on the land. I will give you great harvests from your fruit trees and fields, and never again will the surrounding nations be able to scoff at your land for its famines. *Then you will remember your past sins and despise yourselves for all the detestable things you did*"; italics mine.

8. John 3:8.

9. "For we know that all creation has been groaning as in the pains of childbirth right up to the present time. And we believers also groan, even though we have the Holy Spirit within us as a foretaste of future glory, for we long for our bodies to be released from sin and suffering. We, too, wait with eager hope for the day when God will give us our full rights as his adopted children, including the new bodies he has promised us" (Romans 8:22–23).

10. Dora Greenwell, "I Am Not Skilled to Understand," in *Hymns II*, ed. Paul Beckwith, Hughes M. Huffman, and Mark Hunt (Downers Grove, IL: InterVarsity Press, 1976), 101.

11. Quoted in C. J. Mahaney and Robin Boisvert, *How Can I Change?*, title page.

CHAPTER 18: HARDHEADED LOVE

1. From Cat Stevens' album *Tea for the Tillerman*, copyright © 2000 Universal Island Records Ltd.
2. See Deuteronomy 23:3, 6.
3. This phrase was coined by the eighteenth-century political philosopher Thomas Hobbes to describe the natural condition of mankind.
4. Robertson McQuilkin, *A Promise Kept* (Carol Stream, IL: Tyndale House, 1998), 22–23.
5. *The Lord of the Rings: The Fellowship of the Ring*, New Line Cinema (2001).
6. Lewis Smedes, "The Power of Promises," in *A Chorus of Witnesses*, ed. Thomas G. Long and Cornelius Plantinga Jr. (Grand Rapids, MI: William B. Eerdmans Publishing Company, 1994), 156, italics in the original.
7. Ibid., 157.
8. Cited by Kevin Conrad, *Wisdom for Faithful Living Today*, SermonNotes .com.

CHAPTER 19: COURAGE

1. Patrick Henry Reardon, *Christ in His Saints* (Ben Lomond, CA: Conciliar Press, 2004), 243.
2. Craig Brian Larson and Phyllis Ten Elshof, *1001 Illustrations That Connect* (Grand Rapids, MI: Zondervan, 2008), 276–277.
3. Reardon, *Christ in His Saints*, 243.
4. Ibid., 244.
5. See 2 Corinthians 12:1-10.
6. From *Te Deum Laudamus*.
7. See the chapter on Esther in Raymond B. Dillard and Tremper Longman III, *An Introduction to the Old Testament* (Grand Rapids, MI: Zondervan, 1994), 189–198.
8. "Big Mistake," words and music by David Wilcox, copyright © Irving Music Inc; Midnight Ocean Bonfire Music, 1992.
9. Jean-Pierre de Caussade, *Abandonment to Divine Providence*, trans. John Beevers (Garden City, NY: Image Books, 1975).
10. Cf. Psalm 40:8.
11. C. S. Lewis, *The Abolition of Man* (New York: HarperCollins, 1944), 25.

CHAPTER 20: FINISHING WELL

1. See 1 Corinthians 15:10; Philippians 2:12–13.
2. Karl Barth, *Church Dogmatics* 3, no. 4, ed. G. W. Bromiley and T. F. Torrance (Edinburgh: T. & T. Clark, 1978), 615.
3. Annie Dillard, *Pilgrim at Tinker Creek* (New York: HarperCollins, 1974), 13–14.
4. See James 4:6.
5. See 1 Peter 1:12.
6. A paraphrase of Rubem Alves: "Hope is hearing the melody of the future. Faith is to dance to it."
7. See 1 John 3:2.
8. John Donne, *Divine Poems, Sermons, Devotions and Prayers*, ed. John Booty (New York: Paulist Press, 1990), 80.
9. Buechner, *Wishful Thinking*, 48.
10. Robertson McQuilkin, "Let Me Get Home before Dark," in *A Promise Kept* (Carol Stream, IL: Tyndale House, 1998), 81–82.

Online Discussion *guide*

TAKE *your* TYNDALE READING
EXPERIENCE *to the* NEXT LEVEL

A FREE discussion guide for this book
is available at bookclubhub.net, perfect
for sparking conversations in your book
group or for digging deeper into the text
on your own.

www.bookclubhub.net

*You'll also find free discussion guides for
other Tyndale books, e-newsletters, e-mail
devotionals, virtual book tours, and more!*

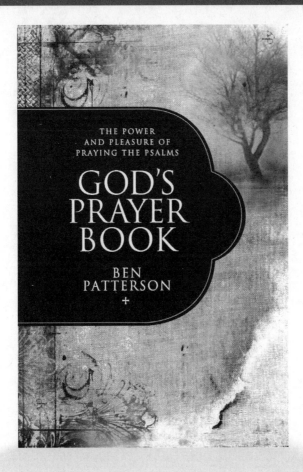